INTRODUCTION TO PSYCHODYNAMIC
PSYCHOTHERAPY TECHNIQUE

INTRODUCTION TO PSYCHODYNAMIC PSYCHOTHERAPY TECHNIQUE

SARAH FELS USHER

International Universities Press, Inc.

MADISON   **CONNECTICUT**

Copyright © 1993, International Universities Press, Inc.

All rights reserved. No part of this book may be reproduced by any means, nor translated into a machine language, without the written permission of the publisher.

First Paperback Printing, 1998

Manufactured in the United States of America

For My Students

Contents

Acknowledgments ix

Introduction xi

1. Understanding the Language of Psychodynamic Psychotherapy. 1
2. Starting Out 27
3. History Taking and Formulation 39
4. Selecting Appropriate Patients 53
5. The Ongoing Therapy. 63
6. Ending 99
7. Special Challenges Patients Present 121
8. Using Supervision 137

References 153

Name Index 157

Subject Index 159

Acknowledgments

I would like to thank Dr. Robert Stevens, at the time a long-suffering student-supervisee, who gave generously of his time to read the manuscript and to offer valuable suggestions. In addition, I would like to thank Sidney Fels whose patient help with the psychologist-computer interaction was invaluable in getting this book written. My husband, Gary McKay, gave constant support throughout and endured many quiet weekends of reading chapters and giving gentle comment.

Introduction

This book is addressed to the beginning student of psychodynamically oriented psychotherapy and is offered as a technical guide to the conduct of this type of treatment. It is certainly consistent with the nature of psychotherapy that therapists must use techniques that "feel" right to them, that make sense to them philosophically, from their own experience of life and relationships, and that fit with their own personality as they experience themselves. Throughout the process of seeing patients and having supervision with different types of supervisors, who may have different theoretical orientations and diverse methods of treatment, each individual therapist will find him- or herself changing and shifting. First one method will be adopted as the "only" one, then another will be tried, until eventually the therapist takes from each supervisory and therapy trial what seems right for them in terms of becoming a consonant psychotherapist.

It is the author's impression that although other forms of psychotherapy, such as cognitive therapy, behavioral therapy, gestalt, and so on, are sometimes equally or more useful for certain patients and feel more comfortable for some therapists, having a grounding in psychodynamic theory and technique can provide a valuable base not only for psychodynamic psychotherapy but also for the subsequent conduct of most of these other therapies. An either–or way of thinking, or a competitive approach as to which method is better, may apply in special cases as therapy is carried out, but really should not occupy valuable space in the beginning clinical student's mind. Take it as a given: Having an understanding of and being familiar with psychodynamic technique will never get you into trouble and will always

INTRODUCTION

be a good base on which to build whatever theoretical approach you may decide eventually to adopt.

The fact that the focus of this book will be on the technique, or the applied part of the process, does not mean to imply, of course, that reading about and understanding psychodynamic and psychoanalytic theory is unimportant. It is generally accepted that both in psychoanalysis and psychodynamic psychotherapy, as in any other scientific endeavor, the relationship between data of observation and theoretical propositions or concepts is extremely important and highly complex (Bibring, 1968). Such theoretical knowledge is an integral part of one's training as a therapist. It feeds that part of you that can intellectualize and hypothesize about what is going on with your patient, as he or she is speaking in the session, and when you think about your patient afterwards. It is this knowledge of theory *and* technique that separates you from untrained "counsellors" of every sort, well-meaning friends and relatives, or the patient's lover. Your theoretical knowledge is something you can sometimes even share, in appropriate doses, with your patient. There are many excellent books on psychoanalytic–psychodynamic theory, and so I will not review here what has been said well elsewhere. I particularly recommend Sandler, Dare, and Holder (1973), Greenson (1967), Volume 1 of Frosch (1990), chapters 1 and 2 of Gabbard (1990), and the section on psychoanalysis in Castelnuovo-Tedesco (1991). Eagle (1984) offers an excellent updated overview of current developments in psychoanalytic theory including object relations theory and self psychology, as do Greenberg and Mitchell (1983) in their book *Object Relations in Psychoanalytic Theory*.

A lot of what will be said in this book is taken from my experiences in supervising doctoral interns in psychology. My method of supervision has been first to review with them the basic concepts of the psychodynamic approach, to discuss a method of

INTRODUCTION

taking the patient's history, and then to ask the intern to tape every session, from beginning to end. I listen to the tape on my own time, making notes on their interventions, and on the flow of the session. During the supervision hour the intern's feelings and impressions of the session are discussed and my notes are fully explained to them. Beginning students often like to listen to the tape once again, with my notes, and raise any matters with me in our next supervision hour that were not clear to them or about which there was disagreement on the student's part. (For some of the material in this book, I dictated my thoughts immediately after a supervision session, which included important points raised by the student therapist.) A more extensive discussion of supervision and its effects on the student will be found in chapter 8.

There are certainly drawbacks to doing supervision in this manner: One is that it is fairly time-consuming for the supervisor, but more importantly, it does not allow for the emergence of as much countertransference material as when the student makes a direct report of the session to the supervisor. When a student tries to describe a session, both the student and the supervisor become aware of the student's affect in telling about certain parts of the interaction and also, of course, in noting what the student "forgot" or "left out." This cannot happen when the supervisor has heard the entire session on tape, at least not in quite the same way. However, it is my feeling, and this has been confirmed by my supervisees, that particularly with beginning students, the amount that can be learned about technique from the method of taping compensates for the aforementioned lack.

Throughout the book I will refer to the objects of our therapeutic endeavors as *patients* rather than clients, only because I received my training in a hospital setting, and this word comes more naturally to me. Clinical trainees, who in my own experience have mostly been doctoral level students in psychology, are

INTRODUCTION

usually referred to as *students*; however, the term is meant to include psychotherapy students, interns, and residents in all related disciplines, most particularly psychiatry and social work.

The goal of this book, then, is to serve as a guide to beginning therapists who want to learn about psychodynamically oriented psychotherapy technique. I hope it will also help them to enjoy the experience of carrying it out.

1.

Understanding the Language of Psychodynamic Psychotherapy

This chapter will offer definitions for some of the more frequently used concepts in psychodynamic psychotherapy, along with a beginning discussion of technique. These definitions may not be entirely meaningful to the reader at this point; however, they are put at the beginning of the book in an attempt to reduce anxiety about terminology and make the rest of the book more immediately accessible to the reader. Interwoven into some of the definitions are beginning suggestions for technique, that is, for working with the concept within the actual therapy situation. This is particularly true in the sections on transference and resistance, as it was felt that these major concepts could be made more understandable in this way.

PSYCHODYNAMIC

The psychodynamic approach is based on psychoanalytic thought and theory that began with the writings of Sigmund Freud. The theory and technique of psychoanalysis as developed by Freud are based essentially on clinical data derived from the study of neurosis, which was originally believed to be basically the study of neurotic conflict (Greenson, 1967). In essence, behavior is viewed as a product of hypothetical mental forces, motives, or impulses and the sometimes conflicting psychological processes that regulate, inhibit, and channel them. The word *dynamic* implies movement; in psychodynamic therapy we are aware, then, that there is a fluid movement of these forces and an ebbing and flowing of the strength of the resistances that arise to modify them in relation to the outside world. As the therapist listens, connections are made between the patient's current thoughts and feelings and his or her past experiences—sometimes very early ones—with the knowledge that many of these experiences have been "forgotten" or repressed and can only be seen in their current, often disguised or distorted, manifestation. These thoughts and feelings of the patient are of central importance in the therapy, then, as it is from them that we infer the underlying inner psychological processes.

In a comprehensive description of the origins and characteristics of the various types of psychotherapies, Frosch (1991, Volume 2) traces the attempts that have been made to distinguish psychoanalysis from psychodynamic psychotherapy. He states that in contrast to psychoanalysis, psychodynamic therapy may achieve more rapid symptom relief, but it also has a wide range of intermediate goals. In both the psychoanalytic and the psychodynamic approachs, the meaning of the patient's symptomatology is sought in the context of an overall picture of the patient as a dynamic, growing, feeling, changing human being with conflicts, fears, anxieties, and psychological defenses. The individual's ability to form close relationships, both within the family and outside it, his or her strengths and weaknesses, preferences for specific psychological defenses, and how these factors shape character, are all part of a psychodynamic approach.

Psychology students who are learning the administration and interpretation of certain psychological tests, particularly the Rorschach, become accustomed to the detective work of discovering what makes the patient tick, and to highlighting the individual's defenses (for example, see Woody and Robertson, 1988). This way of thinking is extremely helpful when meeting the patient in a therapy situation, as you begin to see the defenses in action. It is helpful for beginning therapists (and others, of course) to read psychological reports that describe these dynamics and then to watch for them in the therapeutic situation. Similarly, if you have seen a patient in psychodynamic psychotherapy for some time, you should be able to predict the results of psychological testing, and possibly even some of their Rorschach responses!

Psychodynamic treatment is always based on an understanding of the transference, that is, on the relationship that the patient forms with the therapist (more will be said about this later). To greater or lesser degrees, this relationship becomes the fulcrum for the treatment; in psychodynamic therapy, it should never be ignored. As I mentioned earlier, this book will not undertake the task of describing psychoanalytic theory. The student is strongly urged to read in this area in order to become familiar with the history and development of psychoanalytic thought.

HISTORY

The psychodynamic approach is essentially a historical approach to treatment, meaning that the interpretations or observations made to the patient to help them understand their behavior will be based on the therapist's knowledge of the patient's history (i.e., their early upbringing and family life). It is this, after all, which shapes one's personality. As Basch (1980) put it:

> Throughout our lives we signal implicitly by behavior, appearance, and attitudes the hopes, the wishes, and the fears of childhood which we try explicitly to hide from ourselves and from others by assuming so-called adult roles. Our happiness depends

to a great extent on how successfully we manage to blend those early needs with the expectations we and others have of us as adults. A person who becomes a patient in psychotherapy is saying in effect that in some significant way he or she has failed to achieve this goal [p. 30].

A thorough understanding of the patient's childhood, then, will help us to identify important themes in terms of relationships with significant others, attitudes toward school and work, philosophy of life, and so on. This type of understanding is also invaluable in predicting what will happen in therapy, in terms of the patient's motivation for work, the resistances that may emerge, and, of course, in predicting how the relationship with the therapist will be played out. Therefore, a more or less structured history should be obtained from the patient as close as possible to the beginning of treatment. A suggested outline for the actual history taking will be detailed in chapter 3.

EMPATHY

This is a concept inherent to the conduct of all effective psychotherapy and consists, in essence, of feeling the world from the *patient's* point of view, *not* according to how the therapist thinks the patient should or must be feeling. The definition of empathy, from the Oxford English Dictionary is: "the power of entering into the experience of or understanding objects or emotions outside ourselves." Freud (1921) considered empathy an essential part of treatment. More recently, the psychoanalyst Heinz Kohut (1977), in working with borderline and narcissistic personality disorders, formalized the concept, refocusing therapists' attention on the central importance of empathy. "In psychoanalytic therapy empathy is used to describe an intrapsychic process in the therapist by which an understanding of the patient, particularly an emotional understanding, a capacity to feel what the other is feeling, is enhanced. Situated somewhere between listening and interpreting, empathy serves as a precondition for both" (Berger, 1987, p. 8).

The therapist has, then, to be able to sample, to experience some of what the patient is experiencing, to know what the feeling must feel like *for the patient*, and if not, to be able to sufficiently clarify the feeling with the patient so that what the patient feels is clear to the therapist. The ability to empathize depends partly on the capacity to be able to identify with others. It is not necessarily a natural "talent," although some people do seem to find it easier to accomplish than others, and it can be a learned skill. Even for people to whom empathy comes relatively easily, it is important to know the limits of your empathic ability and to be able to learn to use it as a therapeutic tool. This means being aware of when you are empathizing with your patient; that is, being conscious enough of the process to be able to dip into your patient's feelings at appropriate times in the session and then to step out to your own more objective knowledge and experience at other times. It also means being as aware as possible of your own emotional, countertransference reactions to your patient, particularly when you may be having difficulty in being empathic and when you may be getting "too involved." More will be said about countertransference later in this chapter and throughout the book.

There are times when beginning therapists can go overboard in trying to reflect a feeling back to the patient in an effort to be *really* empathic. One of my interns, for example, when exploring a patient's dilemmas concerning which courses she should be taking to establish a new career for herself, seemed almost to feel more than her patient did about the matter. In one session, the intern, in a pained tone of voice, used the words: "That must have torn you apart," attempting to capture her patient's feelings about the difficulties at school. The patient then said: "No, it didn't feel *that* bad." *Empathic failure* is the term used to describe a "miss," when the patient's feelings were not captured accurately. There can be degrees of empathic failure, from very slight to gross, and most therapists, no matter how experienced, have failures from time to time. When this occurs, it may be noticeable from your patient's verbal reaction, from a facial expression, or from body language (e.g., the patient may move away from the therapist). Depending on the patient and the point that has been reached in the therapy, it is usually best to "admit" to these types of failures immediately and to ask the patient for a further clarification of what they are saying. It is also imperative to discover the patient's reaction to not having been understood.

When the therapist has been able to give an accurate, empathic response, the patient will not only agree in an affective manner, but will continue with the theme, often using the therapist's choice of words, giving several more examples of the theme in an almost excited and sometimes rapid manner, and taking the exploration of the material deeper. Psychotherapy is beginning to be carried out once a therapist is able to step in and accurately touch the patient's feeling, experience it for a moment, and then come "up" again to think about or formulate the feeling in the context of everything the patient is saying and of what is known about that patient.

TRANSFERENCE

This term has been used so often and misused in an almost clichéd manner that it is important to try to get an understanding of it as early as possible. The concept was first introduced by Freud to describe a phenomenon that develops when a neurotic patient is undergoing psychoanalysis. When he first wrote about transference in the *Studies on Hysteria* (Breuer and Freud, 1893–1895), he referred to it as that part of the therapist-patient relationship where the patient makes a "false connection" onto the analyst. In "The Dynamics of the Transference" (1912a), Freud writes:

> It must be understood that each individual, through the combined operation of his innate disposition and the influences brought to bear on him during his early years, has acquired a specific method of his own in his conduct of his erotic life—that is, in the preconditions to falling in love which he lays down, in the instincts he satisfies, and the aims he sets himself in the course of it. This produces what might be described as a stereotype plate which is constantly repeated in the course of the person's life, so far as external circumstances and the nature of the love-objects accessible to him permit, and which is certainly not entirely insusceptible to change in the face of recent experiences [pp. 99–100].

He states that the patient then introduces the therapist into one of the "stereotype plates" formed from earlier times.

Later, in his paper entitled "An Autobiographical Study" (1924), Freud wrote as follows about the transference:

> In every analytic treatment there arises, without the physician's agency, an intense emotional relationship between the patient and the analyst which is not to be accounted for by the actual situation. It can be of a positive or negative character and can vary between the extremes of passionate, completely sensual love and the unbridled expression of an embittered defiance and hatred [p. 42].

Freud described the technique of handling the transference in the therapy situation as: (1) make the transference conscious to the patient; (2) demonstrate to the patient that it is an obstacle to the treatment; and (3) attempt, with the patient's help, to trace its origin in the patient's history (in Greenson, 1967).

The term *transference* refers, then, to both conscious but more particularly unconscious repetitions of early important relationships and can and does occur in any type of psychotherapy, and, in fact, in all of our relationships, to some extent, throughout life. The technique of psychoanalytically oriented or psychodynamic psychotherapy puts it under a magnifying glass where it can be more clearly seen and then analyzed and understood. Transference is actually an inappropriate *displacement* onto the therapist (or misplacement, if you will) of the patient's at least partly unconscious perceptions of figures in their past. In the classical sense, it is not a projection of the patient's current feelings, but a displacement of those feelings that were originally attached to, and are meant for, another significant person, such as the patient's father or mother. The patient experiences as real the feelings, drives, attitudes, fantasies, and defenses toward the present person, in this case the therapist, that actually are the repetition of the early reactions.

The tipoff is that the reaction is always inappropriate. It may be an overreaction to the situation or to the therapist, an underreaction, a bizarre reaction, or even a total lack of reaction where one would naturally expect one. Ambivalence is also a characteristic of transference reactions, where one aspect or dimension of the feeling is always unconscious (Greenson, 1967). For example, the patient may consciously experience in a therapy session only the angry feelings and not the loving ones, or vice versa, in an intense and unidimensional manner, even though both feelings are actually present. Tenacity is, unfortunately, another characteristic of a transference reaction; it may take many interpretations or observations by the therapist and several by the patient to allow for the reaction to ease up.

For example, a 35-year-old female patient of mine, Ms. A, was always a little early for our appointments, and found herself getting somewhat angry if I were a minute or two late, although she would not acknowledge this over several months of treatment. Her feelings finally erupted when we changed our meeting time to 8:00 in the morning and I arrived for our first session a full five minutes late. She said to me in an overly sweet, somewhat sarcastic tone: "Would you prefer to meet at 8:15 A.M. instead?" Responding to the condescension in her voice, I commented that she must be feeling quite angry at me, which turned out to be the tip of a very productive iceberg. (I grant here that a therapist's being five minutes late is, in reality, something to be angry about; however, in this case the feelings seemed overly intense.) During the session, my patient began to recall waiting in the family car as a young child with her mother and sisters, all excited to go out together, while her father, who was somewhat of a tyrant and controlled the women and girls of the family with threats of physical violence, stormed around inside the house deciding whether and when to go. They had spent a lot of time sitting in that car in the driveway, waiting, angry, but also frightened. In this way, then, my patient's anger at my lateness was fueled by a displacement from the past of her anger at her father for always keeping her waiting. In the session, Ms. A, who had been her father's favorite, was finally able to begin an exploration of her feelings of anger toward the father she at once loved and feared, and who was, at the time she entered therapy, suffering from Alzheimer's disease.

There are many ways of classifying the various clinical types of transference reactions; the ones most commonly used being the *positive* and *negative* transference. The *positive* transference refers to those feelings of liking, respecting, being sexually attracted to, and even loving the therapist. Freud (1917) said about the positive transference:

> When a similar affectionate attachment by the patient to the doctor is repeated regularly in every new case ... under the most unfavourable conditions and where there are positively grotesque incongruities, even in elderly women and in relation to greybearded men (*!*) [exclamation mark mine], even where, in our judgement there is nothing of any kind to entice, then we

must ... recognize that we are dealing with a phenomenon which is intimately bound up with the nature of the illness itself [pp. 441–442].

The *negative* transference, as it has classically been defined, refers to some variety of feelings of aggression in the form of anger, dislike, hate, or contempt for the therapist (Greenson, 1967). As was mentioned earlier, most transference reactions that we see in the behavior of our patients are actually a mixture of both reactions, because the nature of transference feelings is that they are ambivalent. It is always interesting to look mentally for the opposite side of the reaction from the one that is currently being manifested. In the example of Ms. A offered above, the ambivalence can readily be seen in exploring the patient's feelings about the original object, her father, as well as in the therapist's sense of how the patient responds currently to being in the treatment relationship, which in this case was in a positive and appreciative manner.

It is a mistake to think that because you are a female therapist say, your patients' transferences to you will always be of a maternal nature or that you may be seen as a sister. The initial response may be sex-linked; however, this will change quickly if the qualities that the patient experiences in you are incompatible with their experience of the parent of that sex. Let us say that you are a woman therapist seeing a patient whose father was experienced as empathic and whose mother was abusive and uncaring. In this case, it is preferable for the predominant transference to be a paternal one; if not, the therapy will be bogged down by defensiveness and resistance. Of course it also has to be kept in mind that transferences often do not remain in exactly the same form throughout the treatment, and many times even throughout the session. Therefore, you can move from "father" to "mother" sometimes in a matter of minutes. In the case where the father was seen as empathic and the mother not, for example, you could be basking in the glow of a father transference until you make an error in attunement or empathic listening to your patient. At this moment, you may switch from "father" to "mother." If you are alert to these possibilities, then it will be easier to frame in your mind what is happening with your patient. To carry the above scenario a little further, it may be with this patient that the maternal (negative) transference will emerge once the patient feels safer with you. Positive transferences usually emerge first, because for most people, they are somewhat less threatening and certainly more socially acceptable than negative ones. However, if negative transference feelings are never expressed in the therapy, this is not a good sign; it implies either a resistance on your patient's part to exploring negative feelings or countertransference signals on your part that imply that the expression of these kinds of feelings toward you cannot be tolerated.

Transference can also occur in a situation that involves the therapist in the patient's current life. An example of this would be a patient who feels angry at the therapist and is afraid to express it, precipitating a fight with their spouse instead. In this case, for that moment, the spouse represents the therapist and becomes the object of the displaced emotions. Whether the "original" anger belongs with something concerning the therapist in the real and current psychotherapy relationship, or to the therapist as a transference figure, the above example still holds.

Students are often concerned that making observations to their patients based on transference manifestations may seem egotistical or narcissistic on their part. For example, if a holiday is approaching, a therapist, knowing about a patient's history with loss and separation and trying to help the patient to understand how their past may get projected on to the therapy situation at this time, might very well ask: "I wonder what feelings you're having about *our* not being able to meet for two weeks?" Or, if a patient is late for a session, or uncommunicative during a session, the therapist, sensing this may have to do with displacements from the past affecting the individual's current feelings in the therapy, might ask: "Do you think you are having any feelings about *me* that are contributing to your lateness/silence?" Or, even more daringly, if a patient suddenly begins an affair with an "understanding person who really listens," the therapist, thinking about the possibility that the patient is acting out feelings stirred up in the therapy might well make the comment: "Do you think this recent affair could have something to do with your feelings toward *me?*" Beginning therapists may cringe at the thought of putting themselves into the patient's feelings or behavior in this central way. However, as, I hope, will become clearer throughout this book, as a therapist you will become important in your patient's life, whether you wish to be or not, and since transference manifestations are usually not intended for the real person of the therapist but are projections or displacements, comments or observations based on these transferences, where the therapist is not afraid to involve him- or herself as a projective stimulus or even as a real person, are invaluable in helping patients to gain insight into their emotions and behavior.

TRANSFERENCE NEUROSIS

Before moving on, I wanted to make brief mention of this term, for the sake of clarification. It will not be used in this book. Transference neurosis, basically, refers to a new form of transference reactions that occurs during intensive therapy, usually psychoanalysis. In this case the analyst, or therapist, and the analysis or psychotherapy become the center of the patient's emotional life and *all* the important features of the patient's neurotic conflicts are relived in the analytic situation (Freud,

1914). Whereas transference involves fragmentary reproductions of attitudes from the past, the transference neurosis actually becomes a constant and pervasive theme in the patient's life, with fantasies, dreams, hopes, and wishes centering on the therapist (MacKinnon and Michels, 1971).

COUNTERTRANSFERENCE

As referred to in this book, countertransference will be used to mean all of the therapist's images, feelings, and impulses toward the patient, conscious and unconscious. Racker (1968) refers to the countertransference neurosis, stating that the therapist is doubly vulnerable in the treatment situation because of playing the role as both interpreter of the patient's behavior and unconscious processes and as the object of these same processes. Of course, conscious reactions are usually easier for the therapist to handle, as he or she is aware of them. These reactions provide the sort of material we sometimes talk to our colleagues about when, for example, we are having difficulty with a particular patient or if we feel like boasting about our accomplishments with a certain patient. Sometimes a part of the therapist's conscious reactions to the patient are responses that pertain to the patient as he or she actually is, and are reactions that most people would have to this patient (e.g., the patient is likeable, funny, etc.). It is when the therapist's reaction seems idiosyncratic, specific to the individual, and may be determined by the therapist's own past, that one has to be extremely vigilant. Of course the therapist is a human being with a history, with fears, anxieties, and strong emotions. Like all human beings, the therapist is subject to prejudice and preference, responding to charm and warmth in patients and feeling uncomfortable in the face of overt hostility and aggression (Slavson, 1953). It cannot be hoped that these responses will not be triggered by one's patients, but only that the therapist will become aware of their possible existence and, for the most part, work them through instead of acting them out.

Positive countertransferences can arise from a number of sources, including the patient representing the therapist's own ego ideal, memories of individuals in the therapist's past, and a need to be liked by one's patients. Some patients seem to work hard in therapy, which fits with the therapist's goals and the need to be successful, and thereby reduces the therapist's anxiety and makes for a more favorable attitude toward those individuals (Slavson, 1953). Negative countertransferences can arise by the patient's activating painful memories in the therapist, or even fear. Resistance to treatment, if it persists, can sometimes evoke negative feelings in the therapist. Overly intrusive behavior on the part of the patient, such as prying into the therapist's personal life, continual criticism of the therapist's manner, clothing, or office, abuse of the opportunity to telephone the therapist, all of these types of behaviors have the potential to stir up a negative countertransference.

It goes without saying that the most destructive countertransference reactions are those that are, and remain, unconscious. Usually the best way for beginning therapists to start to recognize their own countertransference is through the process of supervision. Here, in a relatively safe environment, as you report the details of your session, and as you discuss as many as possible of the feelings and fantasies evoked by the session, you will start to learn what gets to you and what does not, where your own "soft spots" are, and why certain patients trigger certain kinds of responses in you.

For most therapists, especially those who want to pursue a psychodynamic or psychoanalytic approach in their work, individual psychotherapy or psychoanalysis is invaluable. This is the best way to learn about your own personality dynamics and in so doing to understand why you are affected in certain ways when practicing psychotherapy. It also gives you tremendous insight into what it feels like to sit in the other chair: being late for appointments, leaving a session feeling upset, the therapist's holidays and their effects, and the enormous importance of what a therapist says to a patient. If you include psychotherapy or psychoanalysis as part of your training, you will get a real sense of all of these facets of therapy that loom so large for your patients. There is often a noticeable increase in empathic attunement to and in understanding of the patient, as well as therapeutic effectiveness in those therapists who have undergone their own psychotherapy.

WORKING ALLIANCE

The working alliance, or therapeutic alliance, essentially speaks to the element of partnership in the psychotherapy. It describes the relatively nonneurotic, rational rapport which the patient has with the therapist. It is the manifestation of the patient's capacity to work purposefully in the treatment situation (Greenson, 1967). The working alliance is distinct from the transference and, at the best of times, coexists with the transference, so that it can be clearly identified even when the patient is in the throes of a transferential reaction. For example, the patient might be responding to an interpretation as criticism, but may also be able to say: "I feel criticized by you now, but yet I know *you* don't criticize me and I realize that this is the feeling I had whenever my father made comments about my behavior." The patient's motivation to overcome problems, along with a sense of helplessness, and a conscious and rational willingness to cooperate, all form part of the working alliance. In psychoanalytic terminology, the actual alliance is formed between the patient's reasonable ego and the therapist's analyzing ego (Sterba, 1929). Luborsky (in Claghorn, 1976) outlined two types of working alliance: (1) based on the patient's experiencing the therapist as supportive and helpful with himself as the recipient, and (2) the alliance that is based on the working together in a joint struggle, with shared responsibility, for working out the treatment goals. The working alliance, then, is a part of the "real" relationship, for the most part, and tends to develop as the work begins in an almost silent, imperceptible manner. It takes different lengths of time to form for different patients, and may take three to six months for most patients to fully develop. Patients who never develop this kind of alliance, who react solely to the therapist in an instinctive, impulsive, intensely emotional and transferential manner at all times (e.g., some individuals with borderline personality disorders), will be difficult, if not impossible, to treat in psychodynamic psychotherapy. The formation of a working alliance usually requires that the patient identify with the therapist as treater, at least partially and temporarily. Then the patient can begin to work with him- or herself in the same way as the therapist has been working with the patient, so that both of them are moving toward the same goals. However, some patients may use their strong identification with the therapist and their awareness of the technique as a resistance against dealing with more painful and embarrassing material, because they are always striving to be liked or admired by the therapist. Obviously, it is important to try to identify this if it is happening and to point it out to the patient in an appropriate manner at an appropriate time.

In order for a working alliance to be formed, the patient must feel comfortable with the therapist, and so the therapist must play an important role in the formation of this alliance. Winnicott (1945) first introduced the concept of the "holding environment" in describing the environment that the mother provides for the infant within which he is contained and experienced. This term has been seen as an apt descriptor of the therapy situation where it is the therapist who must endeavor to provide for the patient an accepting and safe milieu so that he or she can, for the most part, relinquish the defenses needed in the outside world. Greenson (1967) highlights several of the contributions made by the therapist that reinforce the provision of this environment and contribute to the formation of the working alliance. Certainly the personality, or presentation, and the theoretical orientation of the therapist are relevant and begin to be assessed almost as soon as the patient meets the therapist. The therapist should explain all new or strange procedures to the patient early on. As much as possible, patients should be given regular hours for their treatment; if the sessions are to be held on a weekly basis, they should be held on the same day of the week and at the same time. This helps the patient to organize his or her life around the sessions, and the regularity reduces anxiety and contributes to the impression that important work is going on.

Although it is certainly not advisable to break off a patient in the middle of a sentence, you should try, as much as possible, to end the session at the planned time. Beginning therapists often feel they are giving their patients something by going overtime, but it is my experience that patients, at best, find this confusing in terms of what it means about the therapist's feelings for them and, at worst, find it an inconvenience as it makes them late for the rest of their day. If you as the therapist are late, you should try to make up the time, providing the patient has a few extra minutes to spare that day; if not, the amount to be made up can be carried over to another session, preferably the next one. More will be said about ending sessions in the next chapter and throughout this book. Also, as part of your commitment to your patient, do not answer the telephone during a session unless it is absolutely necessary. If this is the case, you should warn your patient ahead of time that you are expecting an important call and will have to answer. Turning the ringer on your telephone as low as possible, or off completely, if this is feasible, is a helpful way of screening out this unwanted distraction and of letting your patient see that the whole of your attention is focused on him or her. Informing your patient of vacation plans well in advance contributes to the formation of the working alliance by letting the patient know how important you feel the work is. (More will be said about this in chapter 5.) All of these points may seem minor as your read them; however, in practice they are of great significance in helping your patient to develop an enduring working alliance.

INTERPRETATION

Interpretation is an intervention made by the therapist to help the patient clarify and understand the underlying causes of his or her behavior, thoughts, or emotions. In psychoanalysis, interpretation is usually seen as the therapist's ultimate and decisive instrument or tool and every other procedure, for example, empathic reflection, prepares the patient for interpretation, or amplifies an interpretation, and may itself have to be interpreted. To interpret, in its purest sense, means to make an unconscious phenomenon conscious. This can also include the history and source of a given event. By interpreting, then, we go beyond what is readily observable, usually assigning meaning and causality to a psychological phenomenon (Greenson, 1967). An interpretation often requires more than a single mention, and may itself have to be given several times during the course of treatment to be fully heard, accepted, and worked with by the patient. An interpretation usually has two dimensions. In one of these dimensions the therapist makes an *observation* of something unusual or contradictory that the patient has just said, or of a discrepancy in the emotional state the patient is reporting and the way these elements actually appear to the therapist. For example, the therapist might say: "You say you are angry and yet you are smiling." It could be an observation of a *part* of the patient's overt behavior, an example of which might be: "Have you noticed that you've been coming late for the past couple of sessions?" The second dimension of the interpretation is the therapist's attempt to suggest, or hypothesize, a *cause* for the unusual or discrepant statement or for the behavior, by linking it with events in the patient's past or with events in the present treatment situation. To continue with the above example, one might say: "Since we've been talking so much about your mother recently, I wonder if your coming late today was a way of expressing to me what you used to try to express to her by being late coming home every day" (linking the patient's behavior with his or her past). Or, "I wonder if your coming late today has to do with your mentioning at the end of last session that you wanted to talk about sex this time" (linking the patient's behavior with the present therapy situation).

It often happens that our patients are not as impressed with our brilliance as we are, and they do not readily accept our interpretations. (Luckily for us, this too can be interpreted: as resistance, see below.) In addition, lack of acceptance of an interpretation can mean: (1) the interpretation was inaccurate; (2) the therapist's timing was wrong and the patient cannot accept the interpretation at this time, even though it may be accurate; (3) the patient does not understand the language of the interpretation; (4) the patient is a contradictory type of individual and will not accept any interpretation that comes from the therapist; (5) the patient is reacting to the interpretation as if it were a criticism; (6) the patient is in the throes of a transference reaction and hears the interpretation as coming from someone other than the therapist. None of the above are mutually exclusive. The trick is in discovering, step by step, and by testing out your hypothesis again at appropriate times, whether your interpretation was correct or partly correct, or whether you were off-track, and why. Part of this work will be done mentally by the therapist, but a great portion of it can be done in alliance with the patient.

RESISTANCE

Technically, all those forces within the patient which *oppose* the procedures and processes of psychodynamically oriented psychotherapy constitute resistance (Greenson, 1967). Examples of these processes include the patient's motivations to attend therapy and to interact with the therapist, and the patient's attempts to remember and gain insight. Resistances involve the use of the patient's psychological defenses.

Freud, in the *Introductory Lectures* (1917), describes the emergence of resistance in psychoanalysis as follows:

> [S]uch fine weather cannot last forever. One day it clouds over. Difficulties arise in the treatment; the patient declares that nothing more occurs to him. He gives the clearest impression of his interest being no longer in the work and of his cheerfully disregarding the instructions given to him to say everything that comes into his head. . . . He is evidently occupied with something, but intends to keep it to himself [p. 440].

Freud's explanation of why this might occur relates to the patient's transference feelings, either positive or negative, which erupt periodically and get in the way of the smooth progress of the therapy.

Recently, Castlenuovo-Tedesco (1991) has stated that the fear of change is central to the whole analytically oriented therapeutic endeavor and that what presents itself clinically as resistance might productively be looked on as an expression and also a consequence of this fear.

As was mentioned earlier, patients will favor certain defenses, depending on their personality makeup, and it is these defenses that will be observable during times of resistance. Therefore, we would expect the type of patient who uses a lot of denial to be particularly cheerful when resisting an exploration in therapy, commenting that everything in their life seems just fine right now, even though the therapist knows that it is not. A person who tends to use passive aggressive ways of dealing with anger might come late or be silent. A person with narcissistic features might talk about an accomplishment at work or in a relationship, which places him or her in the limelight. These sorts of behaviors will naturally occur throughout the treatment; they can be seen as resistance when they are used, in particular, as an attempt to avoid the procedures and goals of psychotherapy. Resistance may be conscious or unconscious and is usually expressed by emotions, attitudes, behavior, and sometimes a contradiction in emotions versus behavior. In the examples given in the section on interpretation, above, the interpretations were being made of a patient's resistance. Some of the most frequent manifestations of resistance are discussed below.

Whenever a patient cancels an appointment, or misses a session, the therapist must consider the possibility of resistance, no matter how valid the excuse seems. Remembering that resistance may be unconscious, that is, that the patient is not aware of it, resistance must be suspected in all of the following instances in which there are "legitimate" reasons for the patient's behavior: Patients who have very demanding jobs and who telephone at the last minute to say they have been called to an important meeting; patients who take unplanned vacations (i.e., vacations that have not been thought out well in advance and the effect on their therapy considered); patients who get themselves into situations where they are abused and used by family members or friends and thereby miss their sessions. Being late for sessions also has to be suspect, as described earlier, whether the lateness is a habitual occurrence or not. Unusual silences, where the patient "does not feel like talking," may also constitute resistance. Silences in therapy will be discussed further in chapter 5. In addition, when the patient focuses on trivial events or on people's lives outside of the session that have little to do with the patient in reality (e.g., talking about a friend's boyfriend), sometimes called a *flight*, this is also a resistance. A flight can usually best be handled by the therapist saying: "I'm wondering why you're talking about this right now." This type of intervention interrupts the flow and prompts the patient to examine his or her own behavior, and incidentally accomplishes the task of educating the patient about their typical methods of resisting working in treatment. The patient's experiencing "boredom" with the therapy is also usually a resistance, often masking more intense but unacceptable emotions. Acting out outside of the therapy in an attempt to ease the tensions that are building in the therapy relationship, instead of talking about them in treatment, is another common form of resistance for some patients. This acting out may take the form of having a love affair instead of dealing with an erotic transference, or precipitating a crisis or other life change that derails the therapy, for example. Of course, lack of any change at all in those problem areas that brought the patient into therapy is also a resistance, and one that can be extremely frustrating to both the patient and the therapist.

Usually the patient's affective involvement or lack thereof is the tipoff to a resistance. If the patient is overly emotional about something under discussion, if there is little or no affect about a topic that has been seen as important, or if the affect is contradictory or inappropriate to the content of what the patient is saying, these too are cues to possible resistance in treatment.

There are three extremely important areas to be considered in terms of psychotherapy technique when helping your patient to become aware of resistance. (1) *Think about the transference.* As in the earlier example of the patient's coming late to a session, is the patient reacting to the therapist as if he or she were a figure from the patient's past? Resisting may be an indirect way of communicating to the therapist that something is going on in the therapy relationship that needs to be discussed. Whatever the gut sense the therapist has of the transference at this time can be brought to light with the patient, once the observation of the resistance has been made and accepted. (2) *Think about the last session*, that is, the content of the ongoing therapy. Is the present resistance linked to the material of the previous session? An example of this appeared earlier, where the therapist thought the patient's lateness might be related to plans for discussing sex in the next session. Did the patient disclose material that was painful or embarrassing in the previous session, the pursuit of which in the following session might have been very difficult? Or, on reflection, does the therapist think that he or she may not have reacted to certain material as the patient had hoped, that is to say, was there an empathic failure or a disappointing response to particularly charged material? All of this must be thought through carefully and selected hypotheses put to the patient for endorsement or rejection. A third, and also significant, consideration is this: (3) *Think about the resistance in the context of the patient's outside life.* Does the patient tend to be resistant in other close relationships and, if so, at what point does this occur in those relationships: Is it when the patient feels particularly close or warmly toward another? Is it when the patient feels angry? Sexual?

Many beginning therapists resist the encouragement given by their supervisors to comment on their patient's resistance, as they feel the patient will experience these sorts of comments or interpretations as particularly judgmental or critical. However, the suggestion is not to pounce on the patient with an: "Aha! Late again today, eh?" As with all well-timed comments and observations made by a therapist that have been thought through carefully beforehand, interpretations of resistance will be of *help* to the patient, not only in being enlightening about the person's behavior in psychotherapy, but in giving them insight into their behavior in other situations in their life as well.

UNDERSTANDING THE LANGUAGE OF PSYCHODYNAMIC PSYCHOTHERAPY

It is a disservice not to inform the patient when behavior seems to be resistant. By making the observation to the patient that there may be an unconscious reason why, for example, they are late, the patient is taught that: (1) these sorts of issues are important and are the kind of material we talk about in psychotherapy; (2) that the patient does have an unconscious, which is just that, *un*conscious, which does exercise some control over the person's behavior and of which he or she was previously unaware; (3) that in the future when there is an urge to be late for a session, say, the patient can now keep one jump ahead of the therapist by questioning whether or not this is resistance. Patients often do this by making a joke of it; for example, on the telephone they may say to the therapist, "I know you think I'm resisting, but I really can't get out of this important meeting." This is at least one step ahead of where the patient might have been had the therapist not pointed out in a previous session that these types of behavior might signal resistance. The next step, of course, would be for the patient to enter the next session saying, for example, "I figured out that I missed the last session because we were going to talk about my father's death and I found that very painful." Then therapist and patient are actively working together in a productive partnership. If these steps are not initiated by the therapist, they will, in most cases, never be begun by the patient and therefore the patient will never learn about this part of him- or herself.

WORKING THROUGH

This concept is often misunderstood as it is commonly thought of as a one-shot experience that the patient has in either retelling or reexperiencing a past trauma and applying logic to it. However, this is only part of the picture, and this, indeed, is where therapeutic patience becomes a necessity. For working through implies a repetition, indeed *many repetitions* of the process of the patient's understanding or gaining insight into a particular problem. As Gabbard (1990) has said: "Interpretations delivered by the . . . therapist rarely result in 'Aha!' responses and dramatic cures. Typically they . . . require frequent repetition by the therapist in different contexts . . . until the insight has become fully integrated into the patient's conscious awareness" (p. 83). Thus, you, and even your patient, may feel ecstatic when a brilliant insight has been achieved between the two of you that makes the pieces of the puzzle fall together in a way that allows for a fresh understanding of a major portion of your patient's difficulties. But this insight may be "forgotten" by the next session, or it may be altered by the way your patient has thought about it in between or retold it to someone else outside the session. One principle you will learn clearly, over and over again, in the process of doing psychotherapy is the incredible difficulty that human beings have in changing any part of themselves, whether or not that change is seen by them as being for the better. Therefore, what often follows on the heels of insight is resistance. But, take heart: The other principle you will learn is that the issue, if it is important enough, will surface and resurface—all you have to do is wait. Another opportunity will present itself when you can offer the patient the same interpretation or understanding of the behavior in question, maybe from a slightly different angle this time, and then you have *begun* the process of working through. When the issue comes up yet again, try to avoid sighing and thinking to yourself: I thought we'd dealt with this already. What is important here is to understand the context in which the issue has arisen again and why it has not yet been worked through; that is, what are you learning about the nature of the resistance? Successful working through implies that the patient has "finished" work on this problem, or as much as can be reasonably expected considering the patient's and the environmental limitations, and that the understanding gained from this process has become an integrated part of the patient's way of thinking so that the issue is no longer experienced as a problem. One test of whether a problem has been worked through is to ask yourself if your patient were seeking therapy now, would this particular issue be articulated as a problem. If it seems appropriate, you can even ask your patient this question.

2.

Starting Out

Whether this is your first patient ever, or a new patient, there is always some anxiety at this initial meeting. Amazingly enough, you will be able to start taking your countertransference temperature even before the meeting: What are your feelings about being in this particular setting, whether it is a hospital, clinic, or private practice? How desperate were you for a case, or are you already overburdened by the number of patients you are expected to see? What are your feelings about the person who referred the patient—is this a colleague, supervisor, someone known for "good" or "bad" referrals? What have you heard about the patient already and what is your reaction to what you have heard—this includes any demographic data plus the tone of voice of the person giving you this data? What are your feelings, fears, and hopes about the individual who will be supervising you on this case? Do you feel in competition with other students in the setting (e.g., who gets the "best" or "most difficult" patient)? How self-confident are you as a psychotherapist at this point?

As you can see, once you get a referral to see a patient in psychotherapy, many, many factors are already at play. It may seem overwhelming at first that all, or at least some, of the above may be influencing you even before you meet your patient. However, being aware of these possibilities can be of the utmost help.

STARTING OUT

All of the above can be discussed in supervision meetings prior to your first contact with your new patient, and then as they affect you and your relationship with your patient in the ongoing therapy sessions.

THE INITIAL INTERVIEW

Greeting the patient in the waiting room is usually the first personal contact with that person. Addressing the patient by name implies that you have been expecting him or her and makes the patient feel welcome. Next, introduce yourself, so that the patient is sure that this is the right place and the right time. I usually shake hands at this point. Regarding the issue of using the first or last name, it is my feeling that in the waiting room, for the first time, it is always better to use the last name. Once one knows the patient, it is easier to tell which they prefer: this may depend partly on their age, their comfort or discomfort with coming for treatment, and so on. My preference as a therapist has usually been to be called by my last name. This clarifies the relationship as a therapist–patient relationship and not a friendship, and sets some limits which I am usually relieved to have as the therapy progresses. Many interns prefer that their patients address them by their first name, partly because it creates more of a sense of equality and partly because they are not confident enough of their training or skills to put themselves forward as Mr. or Ms. Medical interns and residents in psychiatry more frequently use Dr. with their last name. With psychologists, once they obtain their doctorate degree, they often switch to the use of Dr. from the first-name basis. Maybe being called Dr. seems preferable to being called Mr. or Ms. for some therapists. In terms of greeting your patient, the dictum that the therapist should remain relatively anonymous about his or her personal life does not require you to be unresponsive in the social aspects of the meeting situation. Although you may choose

STARTING OUT

in the interest of treatment not to answer certain questions or engage in small talk, do not be afraid to be friendly when you introduce yourself (Basch, 1980). For example, if a patient comments on the weather or asks how you are today, you should certainly respond appropriately. (Incidentally, in response to the latter, I always answer "fine"; patients do *not* want to know that their therapist is tired, or hassled, or sick.) If you remain silent and do not answer in a normally civilized manner, the patient will feel ignored, imagine you are a very cold person, and will probably feel you already do not like them. The amount of small talk can usually be limited to the time it takes to walk from the waiting room until you are both inside the office. Once in your office, indicate clearly where the patient is to sit. It is best for psychotherapy purposes if the two chairs are placed across from each other at a conversational distance, a little farther apart than would be appropriate in a social situation. The therapist should not sit behind a desk (Basch, 1980).

The goal of a first session is to attempt to make your patient as comfortable as possible so that their problem(s) can be discussed, and, as well, for you to get as clear an understanding as possible about what those problems are. As was mentioned earlier, countertransference feelings have undoubtedly already started to develop. Similarly, transference feelings and resistance on the part of the patient in their unconscious response to the therapy situation and to you as a therapist will be beginning from the first handshake, and, indeed, may have also started developing well in advance of the patient's having made it to the waiting room; the patient's feelings, fears, and hopes about being in therapy, how they got referred to you, their feelings about the hospital, clinic, and so on will all be involved. The following is an example of a patient's feelings about the hospital to which he was coming for outpatient treatment, and the way in which these perceptions affected the course of treatment.

STARTING OUT

Mr. B, a 39-year-old businessman who was seen in therapy by a student I supervised, came into treatment because of rather severe marital problems and interpersonal difficulties with the people at work. He was an extremely anxious, defensive, rigid, somewhat narcissistic type of individual who was not very psychologically minded and was unable to expound clearly on his need for psychotherapy. During the first interview, Mr. B mentioned that his late father, with whom he had developed a very close relationship only as an adult, had been treated at this hospital. This change in the relationship had taken place when he moved back to live with his father when he was in his twenties, after his mother had died. As he spoke about his father, it seemed that there were strong, unresolved loving and caring emotions for him that Mr. B had never been able to express, and which he could even now only vaguely allude to. His father's severe depression had been treated at our hospital on the psychiatric unit; Mr. B stated that his father's psychiatric treatment "saved his life" for a time. Incidentally, he also mentioned that his father had become "friends" with the psychiatrist here. In the beginning of the first session, then, it became evident that his coming to this particular hospital for treatment was of importance, and that he might very well be attempting to identify with his father in this way. As well, there was an obvious, although unstated, expectation that he, too, would become "friends" with his therapist, and maybe that this would "save his life" socially. Unfortunately, probably partly because of the frustration of the latter goal, this patient, who continued in treatment for over two years, never quite succeeded in forming a working alliance with, or making a warm attachment to, his male therapist. Although the interpretation of what might be happening was offered to him on several occasions, he was not interested in working with it. However, he arrived early for every session and his symptoms improved, probably in part because he was able to act out the identification with his father, whom he missed so much, in coming to this particular hospital for help.

In the initial interview, sometimes the patient will begin speaking first, but usually it is up to the therapist to get the interview rolling. What you want to find out is why this patient came for treatment, and there are many ways to ask this that will not put your patient on the defensive. You may have already noticed that your patient has reacted to something in the hallway or your office, that your patient is extremely anxious, that he or she seems to be holding back tears, and so on. These cues will help you in deciding exactly how to begin. I have had first interviews with patients who, as soon as they sat in the chair, immediately began to cry. Just knowing they were in a safe place and that someone was finally there to listen to them and to help them, gave them such a sense of relief that the emotions they may have stored up for a long time came spilling out. "Tell me why you wanted to come and talk to someone"; "Tell me why you wanted to see a psychologist"; "Tell me what's happening with you" are all ways of indicating to the patient that you *want* to know, and are ready to listen. Asking, "Why did you come here" puts patients on the defensive because they may think: Maybe this therapist thinks I shouldn't be here; or maybe I won't be able to express this in the right words to satisfy this therapist.

If you have done your part well, what you will hear next is what is categorized as the *chief complaint* or *presenting problem*. These sorts of labels, although they come from the discipline of medicine and sometimes do not feel appropriate to other disciplines, are extremely helpful in organizing the volume of material you will obtain from the patient and in organizing your thinking as well. For example, Ms. C, a 46-year-old businesswoman, presented to our department with memory problems, complaining that she was unable to recognize faces or recall names of business acquaintances after meeting them, and that she occasionally forgot the names of people she had known for years. Her ability to concentrate was also extremely limited, and she had found herself unable to read books, or even magazines, in the previous four months. She feared she might have Alzheimer's disease. She had been seen by a neurologist and the results of all of his tests had been negative. Still, she was certain there was something organically wrong. In this case, then, the memory disturbance was identified initially as the chief complaint.

The rest of the first session, and maybe part of the next, should be spent on exploring the chief complaint. It is important to know for *how long* the patient has been suffering with this problem; *when* it first started, and *the circumstances* under which it began. Why the patient has come for help *at this time*, is also important. In the above example, if the patient has been noticing memory lapses for the past few years, then obviously it is important for the therapist to know why she has sought treatment *now*. The interview has to be balanced throughout with attention paid to the patient's needs (expressing the nature and details of what is distressing them), and the therapist's needs (finding out relevant information in order to gain a full understanding of the patient's situation and to make an appropriate decision about treatment).

An enormous amount of material can be gathered from this first session if you are able to listen empathically, that is, to hear the presenting problem or problems from the patient's point of view. Beginning therapists are often surprised at how difficult it is to *listen* to a patient. Listening, after all, is not a skill we are ever taught in school; it is something we are supposed to know how to do automatically, provided we do not have a hearing problem. However, in all situations, there are many factors that interfere with hearing what the other person is saying. These factors are magnified in the therapy situation. Student therapists may feel bombarded by the new patient's presentation: how the patient looks; the number of issues that the patient brings up; the sorts of emotions; and the intensity of emotions the patient expresses; and the way the patient responds to the student as a therapist—perhaps by putting themselves totally in their new therapist's hands or by seeming quite guarded. All of the therapist's reactions to these kinds of factors will influence how they listen. Feeling sorry for patients, feeling angry at them, attracted to them, envious of them, or even competitive with them, all starts to happen in the first session and may interfere with the ability to listen to them empathically. Also, although you may enjoy intellectualizing and theorizing about a patient's dynamics, indulging in this exercise prematurely will certainly get in the way of your hearing everything the patient has to say.

Students who have some familiarity with music may find listening to a patient easier because they have been taught to listen to the rhythm and flow of sounds. The therapist must listen both to the words and the music; that is, hear the content of what the patient is saying and try to hear the underlying feelings, or affect, that is attached to the content, as well as what the patient is not saying. This is by no means a passive endeavor; you will be surprised at how much energy good listening takes and at how hard you are working in a session even when you are "just listening." Does your patient seem involved with what he or she is telling you, or detached from it? When certain individuals in the patient's life are described, are changes in affect apparent? If there is no observable affect, then an understanding of this is necessary, and can usually be obtained by involving the patient (e.g., "You're telling me that you are having a hard time dealing with your mother's death, yet you don't express much emotion when you talk about it").

Other important information that can be obtained from the initial interview would include: Does the patient require structure and seem to establish a dependent relationship very quickly (e.g., the patient who says, after telling about their difficulties: "Now I really don't know what to do . . ."—implying, would you please tell me). Most patients want their therapists to like and accept them. Is this the case with your patient, and how is this demonstrated? How does your patient respond when you speak? Does the patient ignore you, or soak up every precious word? It is often interesting in the first interview to try out a possible observation or preliminary interpretation with your patient based on the information they have given you so far, to see how they respond to you and to begin to get a feel for their psychological mindedness. For example, in the case of Ms. C, mentioned above, the interviewer might be able to say: "You tell me your memory disturbance has been worse in the last year since your divorce. Do you think the stress of getting divorced may be having any effect on the problem?" If the patient immediately says "No," this is an indication of possible resistance; if the patient immediately says "Yes," he or she may be too eager for your input and too ready to agree to anything you might say. So what, you may ask, can the poor patient say that is "right"? If a patient reflects on what you have said, considering the possibility, and then agrees or disagrees, this is a more positive sign. If the patient takes what you have said further, for example, by saying, "Well, I guess so. As a matter of fact, the week after the divorce I had the experience of going to a movie and then was unable to remember the story a couple of days later," this might indicate a readiness to think psychologically and to make connections. Once you start to get an understanding of what your patient is talking about, and have taken a complete history of the presenting problem or problems and their effect on the patient's life, then appropriate decisions about treatment can be made.

If your new patient has presented with symptoms of *depression*, then the following questions should be asked to determine the degree or extent of the depression:

STARTING OUT

1. Are you having any problems with sleep? If so, do you have trouble falling asleep; are you waking during the night; do you wake up very early in the morning? When you awaken, what thoughts are on your mind? Are you sleeping more than usual? About how much sleep are you getting most nights?
2. How about your appetite? Does it seem normal for you? Have you gained or lost weight recently? If so, how much?
3. Do you find you are crying more than usual? Does this seem related to anything in particular, or does it just seem to happen for no reason?
4. Do you feel worse at any particular time of the day; for example, early morning, midafternoon, or evening?
5. Do you find yourself thinking gloomy thoughts?
6. Have you felt so bad that you have thought of ending it all—killing yourself?

These questions concern themselves with vegetative, that is, biological, signs of depression as well as suicide potential. If there are strong vegetative signs present (e.g., significant increase or decrease in weight, early morning wakening), then an assessment for antidepressant medication should be considered.

If the patient expresses *suicidal thoughts*, then these have to be explored quite thoroughly to try to determine the probability of their making a suicide attempt. There are questions that are helpful in determining the extent to which these thoughts preoccupy the patient and if he or she has actually made plans to carry out an attempt at suicide: How long have you been thinking this way? How often do you think about suicide? If you were going to do it, how do you think you would do it? If a patient seems to have a clear idea of how they would go about it, then the therapist must go one step further by asking, for example: "And do you have access to pills? Or, to a gun?" The patient's responses to these questions will help you to determine how much danger your patient may be in. Another important determinant is whether the patient has ever made a suicide attempt in the past; if so, they may be more likely to try it again. Under these circumstances, you should ask in detail about the last attempt. If you are concerned that your patient may be suicidal at this time, then you have a responsibility to help that person protect themselves. I might say: "Would you like to come into the hospital for a while?" A surprising number of patients agree, relieved that someone has finally heard how much pain they are in and is going to help them. If you are uncertain as to how to proceed, you can always ask your patient to wait for a while in the waiting room, and try to see your supervisor as quickly as possible.

Because the therapeutic relationship is going to be different from any other relationship the patient has ever had, I like to use the first session as an opportunity to start to *educate* the patient about the process of psychotherapy. I tell them, for example, what can be said in therapy, what is helpful and what is not, and in general, what they can expect from me as well. For example, by stopping the small talk once entering the office, I indicate that this is not what we will be spending our time on in here. By asking how the patient felt coming here, I indicate that it is important to know and understand their feelings about being in therapy. By showing an interest in their relationships, in a dream, if one is mentioned, in all of their emotions and concerns, I show them what we will talk about in our work together. Asking the question: "Anything else?" after a patient has described a problem shows them that you are ready to hear everything. In addition, I will usually give them some information on how often we will meet and how long the sessions will last, as well as a little about the orientation I take to therapy—provided, of course, the patient is not in extreme crisis, and seems receptive to hearing this kind of information.

The way you *end* the first session is extremely important. Again, this will be different from how most people behave in social situations and so the patient will probably have no idea how the ending will come about. You are setting a precedent at this point for the ending of future sessions. Whether or not you have finished finding out as completely as you wanted to about the patient's presenting problem(s), if the time is up: *End on time*. This does not mean cutting your patient off in midsentence, obviously, but it means being aware of the clock and winding down as close to the specified time limit as possible. As was mentioned earlier, you are not doing your patient a favor by going over time. The reliable structure of the therapy situation provides a welcome relief for most patients, even those who seem to want to drag it out. Consistency in ending cuts down on attempts at manipulation, guilt feelings, and the stress for both parties of feeling intruded upon. Be gentle but firm: "Our time is up. We'll continue with this next time." Or, "I can tell this is important for you, but unfortunately our time is up for today." Standing up helps to convey the message that the session is over. There is no need to chat to your patient on the way out or to walk him or her to the elevator, unless the person is infirm and unable to get there alone. Again, this is different from a social situation. Your patient needs some space and some time to think about what has just transpired without your undoing it by being "nice" and walking with them down the hall. More will be said about ending sessions in chapter 6.

Regarding the *taking of notes* during a session, I find it is most helpful to take notes for those sessions in the beginning when you are finding out factual information about the patient; for example, during the very first session and the history-taking sessions. If you do not take notes during these sessions, you may find yourself distracted by the effort of trying to remember details to such an extent that your listening ability will be severely impaired. For psychodynamic therapy, taking notes once the therapy has actually begun is not recommended because note taking is distracting to both the therapist and the patient. I generally advise my patient that I will be taking notes for the first few sessions, implying that this will not be the norm throughout the therapy.

It probably should be mentioned here that once the history notes have been recorded, then you should allow time after every subsequent therapy session for the writing of *progress notes*. These notes consist of a one- or two-paragraph summary of each session, written in the patient's chart, signed by you, and cosigned by your supervisor.

Although in the first session the therapist seems to be getting a sense of a particular patient, often patients can present quite differently when we see them the second time. This may be due to their having been extremely anxious in the first session, or even to something happening in their lives in between sessions. Thus, it is never wise to make formulations based on one session; you can look forward to some surprises in the second session.

3.

History Taking and Formulation

Before starting to take a history in the second session, you should attempt to discover how your patient reacted to the first interview with you. Ask the patient, for example, "How did you feel after our meeting last time?" "Did you have any further thoughts about what we talked about?" Questions such as these will help you to hear about your patient's response to the therapeutic situation and will help your patient to learn what is expected. For example, the patient is expected to think about the sessions in the intervening time and talk about their reaction to them. What happens to the patient in between sessions provides a wealth of valuable material and is an extremely important indicator of their suitability for psychodynamic psychotherapy. Some patients will "forget" what was said by the time they get to the elevator and not give it another thought until you ask them about it. Some patients may have talked to others about what they experienced; one or two may have had a dream about, or related to, the therapy situation. Some may have found themselves more emotional at home or at work. All of this information will help you to begin to see your patient's motivation for treatment, defenses and resistances, their characteristic way of

HISTORY TAKING AND FORMULATION

reacting to new situations, and so on, and, as was stated earlier, to determine the best choice of treatment.

Transitions in therapy are extremely important to the patient, and so it is always necessary to try to make these transitions as smooth as possible. Telling the patient what you are planning to do is a simple way of effecting this, and it works every time. Comments like: "Now I'd like to ask you some questions about your family background"; or "I'd like to ask about your early family life, if that is all right with you," will help the patient to be prepared for what is about to take place. If the patient has any qualms (e.g., "I don't like talking about my family," or, "I'm afraid I don't have a very good memory for those sorts of things") they can be stated and dealt with by reassurance and by introducing questions in a more gentle manner. Most patients will simply nod in agreement and try to answer as best they can. Again, this part of getting to know the patient requires that you write notes, as there will be too many details to remember.

It should be noted here that there are many experienced psychotherapists, particularly psychoanalysts, who prefer not to take a formal or structured history, but to allow the material to flow from the patient in the order in which it occurs to him or her. This is an acceptable way of proceeding after one has taken many, many histories and has a clear idea of exactly what facts are needed about the new patient to determine appropriate treatment. However, for the beginning or intermediate student or practitioner, a good history is invaluable, not only for decisions about the type of treatment but in getting to know your patient early on and in getting a sense of his or her experience in life thus far. What follows, then, is an outline of frequently asked history-taking questions. Many supervisors have their favorite questions; these can always be added to what has been provided below.

HISTORY TAKING AND FORMULATION

The *history taking* usually starts with the patient's parents; you can pick either the father or the mother, and move on from there:

1. *Father*:
   (*a*) How old is your father? Is he in good health? (If he has *died*: What from? How old was he went he died? How old were you when he died? Can you remember your reaction? How long did you feel that way?)
   (*b*) What kind of a person is/was your father? Can you describe him to me? (If the patient has trouble, I may prompt by saying: Was he an outgoing type of person or a quiet person?)
   (*c*) Did you feel close to your father when you were growing up? Did you ever do things with him—just you and him? Did you ever tell him your worries about school or your friends?
   (*d*) Do you have any early memories that involve him that you could tell me about?
   (*e*) What is your relationship like with him now? How often do you see him/speak to him on the telephone/write to him? What is it like for you when you are with him now?

2. *Mother*: The same questions can be asked here as above.
3. Tell me a little about your *parents' marriage* as you saw it:

   (*a*) Would you say they had a happy marriage? Did they fight often? Did you ever see them fight? Did you ever see them express affection toward each other? What was you reaction to these events when they occurred?
   (*b*) Who seemed to make more of the decisions in the marriage?

HISTORY TAKING AND FORMULATION

4. *Siblings*:

    (a)   How many brothers and sisters do you have?
    (b)   Where are you in the lineup?
    (c)   Who is the oldest sister/brother? How old is he or she? Is he or she married? Children? What does he or she do? What is he or she like as a person? What was your relationship when you were growing up? What is your relationship like now? How often do you see him or her, and so on.

This line of questioning should be followed through with every sibling.

5. Were there any *other relatives* who were very close to you—an aunt/uncle or grandparent? Was there anyone else who lived in your home with you? If so, tell me a little about them, and your relationship with them.

6. Now I'd like to ask you some questions about your *school life*.

    (a)   Did you like elementary school?
    (b)   Did you like high school?
    (c)   What subjects did you do well in at school?
    (d)   Did you have many friends at school? Any of them close? Did you have one close friend for any period of time?
    (e)   How far did you go in school?

7. At what age did you *leave home*?

    (a)   Can you tell me what that was like for you?
    (b)   How did your parents react to it?

HISTORY TAKING AND FORMULATION

- (c) Where did you go to live at that time?
- (d) In what circumstances are you living now? How long has that been? Do you like it?

8. Tell me about your *working life*.

- (a) How many jobs have you had?
- (b) Which jobs did you like/not like?
- (c) Why did you leave the jobs you left?
- (d) What job are you doing now? How long have you been in this job? Do you like it?

9. Now I'd like to ask a little about your *relationships* with men/women.

- (a) For *women*: First, could you tell me when you first started menstruating? What was your reaction to it? How is it for you now?
- (b) For *heterosexual* patients: Tell me about your boyfriends/girlfriends. Can you tell me about your first boyfriend/girlfriend? How long did that relationship last? Was that a sexual relationship? How did it end? This line of questioning should be carried through with all subsequent, relatively long-term relationships (six months or more).
- (c) For *homosexual* patients, if it has been made clear already that they are homosexual: When did you first know you were homosexual? How did you react to this discovery? What about your family—do they know? How has it been for you in terms of finding relationships? Can you tell me about some of your more important relationships? How long did the relationship(s) last? How did it/they end?

HISTORY TAKING AND FORMULATION

(d) Are you currently involved with anyone? Tell me about that.

10. Have you ever seen a *psychologist, psychiatrist,* or *social worker* before?

(a) Can you tell me the name of the person you saw?
(b) How long ago did you see them? For how long did you see them? How frequently did you see them?
(c) Why did you stop seeing them?
(d) If appropriate: Did you consider seeing them again this time?
(e) If appropriate: Have you ever been on any medication for emotional problems? Are you now?
(f) If appropriate: Have you ever been in a hospital for a psychiatric/psychological problem?
(g) Has anyone in your family ever sought help for emotional problems? Has anyone ever been hospitalized for this reason?

11. Do you have any serious *medical* problems? Are you on any medication for a medical condition?

12. How about your use of *alcohol.* Do you drink; how much? Do you ever use any street *drugs?* Have you done so in the past?

13. Is there anything I haven't asked you that you think I should know?

If your patient has presented with symptoms of depression, then if you have not asked the appropriate questions outlined in chapter 2 in the first session, you should ask them during the history-taking session.

Mental status is often a part of the history-taking interviews, particularly for residents in psychiatry. This involves getting a sense of the patient's mental competency, from whether or not

HISTORY TAKING AND FORMULATION

there are gross memory problems or a psychotic process in evidence to the patient's intellectual ability and potential for psychological mindedness. There are standard questions that can be asked to determine the former (e.g., asking the patient to try to remember four objects from the beginning of the interview until the middle or end of the interview; asking the patient about delusions and hallucinations) which will not be outlined here as this book concerns itself with psychodynamically oriented psychotherapy. In terms of intellectual ability, usually some sense of this can be obtained from conversing with the patient and from a knowledge of their educational pursuits. Psychology interns who have done a lot of intelligence testing may be able to get a feel for a patient's intellectual functioning more easily than students who have not had this experience. It is important to attempt to establish what intellectual range you believe your patient would be in: average, below average, above average. Potential for psychological mindedness involves, in part, having an initially positive response to the treatment situation and an interest in reflecting on and understanding one's life problems, rather than a focus on what to *do* about them. It was discussed briefly in chapter 1 (section on interpretation) and also at the beginning of this chapter when the patient's reaction to the first session was mentioned, and it will continue to be raised as an issue throughout this book.

Gathering all of this information may well take two to three sessions. Although of course you do not want to dominate too many sessions with your agenda, it is usually important to take as complete a history as possible. You will be thankful later in the therapy when your patient refers to family members and early relationships that you have done so. If your patient comes to a planned history-taking session in a crisis, then you must, of course, work with them concerning the crisis. But remember to *come back* to the history. Asking questions about a patient's history is not as much of a burden to the patient as it may seem; it often helps to communicate to him or her that you are interested in all the details of the person's life, past and present, and that you care enough about what they have been through so far to take the time to ask about it.

FLAGGING THE TRANSFERENCE IN THE HISTORY

Many of my students will be sure that the above heading contains a typographical error, and that what was meant was *flogging* the transference, since they often feel that I pound away at them about transference issues. However, what I mean by flagging is simply putting up a flag—as you might picture on a golf course—so that the particular statement, or emotion, is marked for future reference. During the process of answering questions in the history-taking sessions, your new patient will unknowingly be revealing possible future transference reactions that will arise during the treatment. The questions about father and mother, for example, give an indication of the patient's earliest relationships and whether they were experienced as supportive or critical. Since the psychotherapist is often seen as a parent figure, it is crucial to get an understanding of the perception of each parent by the patient. Then, you may be able to get a sense of which parent you may be representing in the beginning; ideally it is the "good" parent, or the one the patient felt closest to, as it is generally easier to start psychotherapy with a positive transference. However, this may not be the case, or this may change over the course of the therapy. If you are familiar with this part of the patient's history, you will be able to identify these transferences and help your patient to see and understand them as well. If a parent has died, the patient's answers to your questions will give you an indication of whether they have been able to let go of the parent, or may now be searching for a replacement, and also how the patient deals with loss, separation, and so on, which has indications for your own separations—vacations and eventual termination.

Be alert to a possible sibling transference, as well, particularly if your patient is close to you in age.

For example, a 25-year-old single woman, Ms. D, came for treatment complaining that she had very low self-esteem, that everyone in her family criticized her, and that she could not make career or relationship decisions. In fact, she had taken several courses but did not know what she wanted, and had had several relationships with men where she felt she was taken advantage of. During the history-taking session, she described a relationship with her older sister whom she thought of as perfect. This woman had planned her own career and, as well, was almost engaged to a man she had been seeing for some time. During family gatherings, and indeed at almost every opportunity, the sister would tell Ms. D what she should be doing with her life and berate her for being unable to have a career or a steady boyfriend. The patient dreaded these family get-togethers and was at the point of being unable to attend them. She was seen in therapy by a female psychology intern, close in age to herself. The possibility of a sister transference was in evidence as soon as the material about the sister was elicited in the history session. Indeed, this is what developed and a great deal of the therapist's time, particularly at the beginning of treatment was spent in helping Ms. D to observe when she felt she was being judged by her therapist. As she began to see this more and more, Ms. D was able to disclose more unflattering parts of herself and begin to understand them. She started attending family gatherings again, and one of the major accomplishments she achieved in this relatively short treatment was that she was able to stand up to her sister and in the end to reclaim her as a friend.

Hearing your new patient's child's eye view of their parents' marriage will give you a sense of how the patient sees relationships in general, and particularly relationships with the opposite sex. Unresolved oedipal issues, which will emerge in the transference, can often be spotted first in the patient's description of the parents' marriage (e.g., "My father never seemed to talk much to my mother; in fact, he shared more with me—we thought more alike," if spoken by a female patient may herald seductive behavior in the transference with a male therapist and competitive behavior in the transference with a female therapist). The patient's view of adult loving and caring which was born from these early perceptions may reappear in their perception of the therapist–patient relationship.

How your patient accomplished the developmental task of leaving home may speak to dependency–independency needs in the relationship with the therapist. Guilt feelings related to that separation may reappear in treatment; tendencies to cling onto parental figures will also most certainly show themselves. Does the patient have to get angry to effect a separation? If so, no doubt this will happen at some point in treatment.

Issues pertaining to current sexual relationships, your patient's view of men and women, sexuality, and their own attractiveness will unfold as the psychotherapy progresses, whether or not you are in an opposite-sex patient–therapist combination.

FORMULATION

The word *formulation* strikes terror into the hearts of many clinical students, and, unfortunately, sometimes into the hearts of more experienced psychotherapists as well. Because of this, thinking through a formulation is often a task that is avoided. However, as anyone who has been forced to do it will testify, it is an extremely helpful process as it focuses the therapist's thinking on the psychodynamics of the patient and is imperative in terms of making treatment decisions. It will increase your power of predictability and cut down a *little* on the surprises in store in

HISTORY TAKING AND FORMULATION

your subsequent treatment with this patient. Basically, a formulation is a hypothetical explanation of the factors that have contributed to the precipitation, development, and maintenance of your patient's problems, as well as his or her psychological strengths and vulnerabilities. Formulations do not have to be essays and are certainly not *carved in stone*. Because you may have written what you thought was a brilliant analysis of your patient after seeing him or her three times, you do not have to, and should not, adhere rigidly to the same perceptions of the patient's dynamics through the ensuing months or years of psychotherapeutic treatment. In most instances, you will not be put on trial to defend your initial impressions. All of this is said in an effort to reduce whatever formulation phobia you may be experiencing.

As was stated earlier, formulations are basically hypotheses, well thought out hypotheses, that sum up the impression you have gained thus far of your patient. They involve a clear statement of the presenting problem or chief complaint; a summary of its history; and a hunch, or hypothesis, about why this patient is suffering from this complaint at this time (predisposing factors). If appropriate, the formulations include a statement about additional complaints that might be expected to arise for this patient knowing their history; a statement about the personality type of the patient, including, if possible, the type of psychological defenses this patient tends to use; and an estimate of their intellectual and psychological capabilities. You should also include any comments you can make at this point about expected transferences or resistances, recommendations for treatment, and the reasons for your choice of this type of treatment. Residents in psychiatry are also required to postulate a diagnosis, utilizing the most current edition of *The Diagnostic and Statistical Manual of Mental Disorders* (at the time of writing DSM-III-R [APA, 1986]). Because specific training in the use of the DSM for making a formal diagnosis is a standard part of clinical psychiatric teaching in every setting, it will not be outlined here.

If you have listened to and understood your new patient's presenting problems, have a fairly good grasp of the climate in which they spent their early life, and have flagged several possibilities of what might be played out in the transference as you were taking the history, the formulation will almost write itself. It may be helpful, at this point, to offer a couple of examples of formulations.

Ms. C was the 46-year-old woman mentioned earlier who presented with a four-month history of memory problems. The death of her mother three years prior to her coming for treatment and her divorce of six months previous appeared to be recent precipitating factors. It appeared that her memory problems were functional in nature, related to the anxiety she was experiencing due to her unresolved grief over these losses. Her defenses appeared to include intellectualization and somatization. She was of above average intelligence and, once accepting that she should see a psychologist and not a neurologist, had become interested in exploring the roots of her problems, although she remained somewhat concrete in her thinking. A psychodynamically oriented psychotherapy approach was recommended.

In the above example, it was discovered later on in treatment that the patient had been a victim of sexual molestation. However, since this was not known at the time of the formulation, it obviously could not be included in it, and whatever effects it may or may not have had on the presenting problem could not be discussed.

As another example: Ms. D was a 25-year-old single woman who presented with the problem of significant difficulties in relationships. She felt, as well, that her achievements did not measure up to those of her older siblings, in particular one older sister to whom she constantly compared herself. Her feelings of low self-esteem in relation to men appeared to be connected to her experience of her cold and critical father leaving the family home when Ms. D was 16 years of age. She was able to express a fantasy that he left because he did not love her and, in fact, wished that she, the last of four children, had not been born. Although she stated that she had felt quite depressed after her initial interview here, she had been able to think about what she had discussed and seemed more relaxed in the next session. Her affect was quite labile throughout the assessment; she cried and laughed easily and also expressed some "nervousness." From what could be seen so far, Ms. D used denial and attempts to distance herself from painful situations as defenses for coping with her anxiety. She was of above-average intelligence and had a good capacity for insight. Weekly psychodynamic psychotherapy was recommended. It was predicted that a sibling transference would emerge early in the treatment as Ms. D was struggling to define herself against her image of a "perfect" older sister.

Again, in the above case, there was a great deal of information that was not known at the time of formulation. The above examples represent rather concise formulations; they can certainly be longer, but there is no need to reiterate in the formulation everything that has been said in the history taking.

4.

Selecting Appropriate Patients

As you move toward the process of making a formulation on your new patient, one of your considerations will be a recommendation about treatment. Since this book focuses on psychodynamic therapy, let us examine those patient characteristics that give us the most optimism about recommending psychodynamic or psychoanalytically oriented treatment. As was mentioned in the two preceding chapters, a considerable amount of information can be obtained about the patient in the first one or two interviews, and it is from this information that you, in discussion with your supervisor, must make your decision about the most propitious type of treatment. Bearing in mind that your own reactions (countertransference) to your new patient, both conscious and unconscious, will already be underway, it will be important to acknowledge these as you make treatment decisions. Our first responses, in fact, sometimes linger for a long time, sometimes throughout the treatment. Thus, a feeling that you do not like a patient when you first meet should be taken into account when considering more intensive psychotherapy with that patient. If, in discussion with your supervisor, you can get an understanding of why you reacted the way you did, this will obviously be extremely helpful to both of you in making an appropriate decision. Also, considerations about identifying transference issues as they can be predicted from the initial interview and the history taking (see previous chapter) will provide vital information for your choice of treatment.

Psychodynamic psychotherapy, first and foremost, requires that a patient be able to tolerate a somewhat *unstructured* therapy situation. Unstructured therapy occurs when the topic or issue to be discussed in each session is usually raised by the patient, and when the therapist, although offering guidance and interpretations at appropriate moments in the session, generally follows where the patient leads. In essence, this means that the therapist does not use questioning, homework assignments, goal-setting, or other methods of deliberately imposing a structure. Since responses from the therapist are kept to a relative minimum (that is, relative to other forms of therapy such as cognitive–behavioral therapy, but not as minimal as in psychoanalysis), the patient must have some ability to be self-sustaining and not require constant input and approval from the therapist. All of these comments are necessarily somewhat unspecific as it is difficult to say exactly how large a dose of this or that particular intervention is warranted. It is probably helpful just to think of psychodynamic therapy as leaning in a direction *away* from providing structure for the patient.

If your patient appears to be able to tolerate the moments in your initial sessions when you are not asking a question, this is a good indicator that they may be able to tolerate a less structured therapy situation. Typical of these moments would be occasions of silence or the moments when you have put out a feeler, for example, about something they have described in their early life or about a dream they have mentioned, to see if they can discuss it further without needing an immediate solution or resolution.

Another factor one always tries to assess in the opening sessions is the patient's level of *psychological mindedness*. As has been

SELECTING APPROPRIATE PATIENTS

mentioned previously, this means that the patient can hypothesize about his or her own life and show an interest in gaining an understanding of it, again without necessarily needing quick solutions. It also means that the patient has an interest in their family history and its impact, and a generally positive attitude toward being in psychotherapy and toward learning to think in a psychological manner. Patients who have never been in treatment before naturally differ in their familiarity with psychological terms and psychological ways of thinking. However, it is not the patient's ability to offer us a polished presentation of psychological theories we are speaking of here, but rather the ability to philosophise, to entertain new thoughts about themselves, to allow the important role of the past in determining their present difficulties, and an open-mindedness about exploring life in a new way.

GOOD SIGNS

In addition to trying to sift out the kind of information just described above, as well as attending to those relevant factors already mentioned in the two preceding chapters, I would like to offer the following more specific criteria for the intern to keep as *part* of his or her armamentarium when attempting to make the decision about psychodynamic treatment. These criteria are not to be regarded as carved in stone; however, the more of these characteristics your new patient has, the more likely it is that he or she will be a good candidate for psychodynamic psychotherapy.
 (1) The patient should *not* show signs of psychotic symptomatology (i.e., delusions, hallucinations, paranoid thoughts, etc.).
 (2) The patient should be at least average intellectually as estimated by their level of education (in most cases at least high school is preferable), their occupational level, their interests, and

their general knowledge. (3) The patient's general level of functioning should be taken into account (i.e., how are they coping in spite of their symptomatology and will they be able to "wait" for the effects of a psychodynamically oriented treatment). (4) The patient should be interested in the treatment and, at least consciously, express a willingness to cooperate with it. (5) Past relationships should include at least one positive close and caring attachment (e.g., mother or father, a grandparent or close relative). (6) It is helpful if the patient has shown some degree of ability to form a close relationship in the present (i.e., a friendship). (7) The patient should have at least some awareness of their affect or feeling states during the initial interviews and be able to acknowledge and discuss them to some extent. (8) The patient should show some ability to delay impulses and to postpone immediate gratification, that is, to discuss rather than act. This can be discovered in your questioning about how the patient has handled other crises in the past and what thoughts they have had so far about dealing with their present situation. (9) If your patient has memories, dreams, and fantasies relatively available for discussion, this is always a nice bonus, and usually a good predictor for psychodynamic therapy, provided they are not too readily available as in patients who are becoming psychotic. (10) If your patient has had previous treatment, it is better prognostically if they feel the earlier treatment helped them. (11) The patient should not, in the present, and preferably not in the immediate past, be or have been involved in substance abuse or illegal behavior.

Mr. K, a 29-year-old architecture student, came to see me because he was having trouble controlling his angry outbursts. He stated that he was too critical of his wife of one year and that he found himself in a stormy frame of mind almost every time he entered their home. No physical violence was involved. An only child, Mr. K stated that he felt he had been angry for most

SELECTING APPROPRIATE PATIENTS

of his life but was uncertain why. In the history-taking session, he described his mother as a depressive, clinging woman, who made him feel guilty most of the time. He had spent a lot of his childhood worrying that his mother might die; she often said to him when he was naughty: "You'll be sorry when I'm dead." In fact, the mother had been treated for depression with medication at several times during the time that he was growing up. Mr. K remembered a warm and friendly relationship with his father. He felt his father approved of him and loved him. His father often implied to him that the two of them had to watch over the mother and not cause her too much trouble as she could easily become ill. He sensed that this had something to do with his attitude toward his wife who, although she was a healthy young woman, was quite passive in her manner, which enraged him at times.

In this example, all of the above information was obtained from the patient in the first two sessions. His complaint of angry outbursts caused me to proceed with some initial caution. I followed it up with several questions designed to assess his impulse control. He answered my questions in what seemed like an open manner and volunteered information spontaneously in both sessions. He was intelligent and able to articulate his concerns. He did not blame his wife but took responsibility for his anger. He was able to see that his relationship with his mother might have some bearing on the problem. He had had a close and trusting relationship with his father. Finally, he did not expect a "quick cure." I therefore offered him psychodynamically oriented psychotherapy.

BAD SIGNS

As has been mentioned above, the possibility of success in a psychodynamically oriented treatment is much less likely if your patient is having symptoms that indicate possible psychotic thinking in the present or the immediate past, or if there is the possibility of an underlying psychotic process. If this cannot be clearly ascertained in the first few interviews and you are really in doubt as to whether your patient could tolerate an unstructured therapy, then it would be a good idea to refer the patient for psychological testing, particularly projective testing. If you yourself are a psychology intern, it is not a good idea to test your own patient. This complicates the relationship by introducing a new dimension which may well prove to be aversive to the patient. Therefore, after discussing the possibility of testing with your patient, a referral to a colleague is in order. No matter what your discipline (e.g., psychology, psychiatry, social work), it should be understood between you and your patient that the consulting psychologist will discuss the results of the testing with you, in addition to giving your patient feedback.

If your patient does not appear to fulfill a majority of the criteria mentioned at the beginning of this chapter, chances are you will have difficulty carrying out psychodynamic treatment, at least at the start. Sometimes, after several months of the benefits of a structured and supportive therapy, patients can become more able to tolerate less structure and can learn to become more psychologically minded. Often interns are in a hurry to get started with a case and so may be a little lax in applying the criteria for selecting an appropriate patient (Baker, 1980). However, in the interests both of your patient's well-being and of your learning, and also in the interest of avoiding narcissistic injury to your vulnerable self when your patient terminates therapy prematurely, it is best to bear in mind the guidelines given above.

I want to describe an example of a case where the treatment decision was somewhat difficult. Ms. L, a 31-year-old engineer, came to see me saying she wanted long-term psychotherapy. She complained that she was completely isolated from her colleagues, had no friends, and had never had a boyfriend. These

SELECTING APPROPRIATE PATIENTS

social difficulties had been characteristic of her for as long as she could remember. She stated that no one had ever liked her from primary school onwards. Her coming for treatment at this time was precipitated by an incident at work where someone she had thought was going to be her friend, at last, had started actively avoiding her. Ms. L's background was extremely deprived both financially and emotionally. Her parents, who were immigrants, did not allow her to express herself at home and felt that she should not associate with the other children at school, and the latter soon began to tease and even physically abuse her for being different. Her father was also physically abusive to her for no apparent reason. Her mother, who remained distant from her throughout, blamed her whenever anything went wrong in the household in an attempt to deflect the father's anger from herself onto the patient. Ms. L was not allowed more than one or two toys at home, her parents' rationale being that she was an only child and therefore might become spoiled easily! Ms. L was cooperative and spontaneous in her presentation with me, but remained fairly flat in her affect, with the occasional laugh, when discussing very sad and painful past events. Although she stated that she knew her current problems with other people arose from her abusive treatment by her parents, some of her thoughts about how others felt about her had a paranoid flavor.

Again, all of the above information emerged during the first two interviews. Ms. L was clearly intelligent and wanted to cooperate with the proposed treatment. She showed some intellectual understanding of her current difficulties. Yet, I was extremely cautious about the possibility of pursuing a psychodynamic approach with her. Since her past relationships had been so impoverished, I was not at all certain that she could form an alliance in therapy without a significant amount of feedback from her therapist, or that when the going got tough, she could really believe that this was truly a relationship she could trust. I felt that her lack of awareness of her feelings showed a brittle defensiveness and that decompensation might ensue should her defenses be challenged. In terms of the possible transference, I kept in mind that since there was no precedent in her life for a relationship with a positive, caring parental figure, the chances were that the more intense the transference became, the more rage, humiliation, and pain would be mobilized which would be displaced onto the therapist. This would make it more and more difficult for the patient to tolerate remaining in the therapy, and perhaps for the therapist to maintain a neutral, accepting stance. I therefore decided that she needed a structured approach, at least for the first several months or more, with fairly active involvement on my part, not in terms of deciding agendas for her but in being genuinely responsive to her and in role-modeling a positive, relatively nonthreatening relationship.

Once a decision has been made to attempt a more psychodynamically oriented treatment, I often give the patient some vague indications of how to proceed, for example, by saying: "From now on, I'd like you to talk about whatever you feel is important, or about whatever comes into your mind during our sessions." It is usually not helpful to give more specific instructions like, "I'll be interested to hear all about your dreams," as this obviously will bias the patient either to bring in material he or she feels you want to hear or will let them know what will constitute effective resistance in the sessions. The process of starting the psychotherapy is elaborated in more detail in the next chapter. If there is going to be a more drastic change in my approach, then naturally I would explain clearly to the patient what the therapy or the disposition will be, and as much about the reasons for it as I think would be helpful to them. Examples of such a change would be if I were going to launch into a highly structured behavioral approach which required

SELECTING APPROPRIATE PATIENTS

that the patient be informed of all the details of the process, or of course, if I were going to refer the patient to someone else for treatment.

Having said that sometimes a patient can move from a more structured and supportive psychotherapeutic approach to a more unstructured, psychodynamic approach after some time in treatment, I would also like to mention briefly here a different category of patient. These patients will look good on all the variables described earlier in this chapter and you will decide on treating them psychodynamically, but they will turn out *not* to be what they seemed as you get into the therapy. This may happen, for example, with patients who fall into the category of borderline personalities who were not able to be diagnosed earlier, with some narcissistic personality disorders, or with patients who encounter an extreme crisis situation (e.g., a marriage breakup) shortly after starting treatment. This situation often feels like a major disappointment for students, and sometimes for supervisors as well, who feel the patient has let them down. Depending on your setup for supervision, this discovery after several weeks of therapy may at first seem to present serious problems. For example, in some instances the case has been selected for taping, the student has elected to pay for supervision on the case, or the student has selected a particular supervisor because of their approach, and wants to use the case to learn this approach.

If it is not feasible to switch cases for supervision purposes, that is, to carry on with the first case in a supportive manner and find another case for psychodynamic supervision, then you and your supervisor will have to use the more supportive, structured case as a learning instrument. This can be done by discussing the issues of transference and countertransference as they arise during your supervision time and by making psychodynamic formulations with your supervisor. The same issues will

SELECTING APPROPRIATE PATIENTS

always be present in the therapy session, no matter what kind of therapy you are doing and whether or not you choose to bring them to light with your patient. As long as you are aware of your patient's limitations, you can even try out interpretations, provided you are ready to let them drop should they not be picked up by the patient. Bear in mind that any therapy situation with any patient can be a fruitful and exciting learning experience.

5.

The Ongoing Therapy

After the major introductory work has been accomplished, there is another *transition* from the relative structure of the beginning and history-taking questions to the point when the patient is talking about whatever comes to mind. This is often a difficult transition for patients to make because the structure that the therapist has necessarily imposed usually feels safer, and answering questions is usually easier than generating one's own material, at least at first. Again, I tell the patient what is happening (e.g., "I've got enough of this kind of information for now, so next time I will just expect you to talk about whatever you want"; or, "I'm going to put away my notes right now, and for the rest of the time I'd like you to talk about whatever comes to your mind"). There may be a little natural silence as the patient makes the shift to try to adapt. If a patient is really struggling (e.g., "I don't know what to say"), I might comment empathically that this is difficult, or I might ask why it is so difficult, depending on the patient. Talking about the transition usually helps it to occur without the patient having to work at it. Sometimes this is an appropriate opportunity to educate the patient in what is expected (i.e., that he or she will talk and you will listen and try to help them to get an understanding of their difficulties). One can always say, several times if necessary: this is *your* time. This may be a difficult concept for some patients to really grasp, as they may feel on some level that they are here for you, to perform and be a good patient, associating therapy with school or with family situations.

If the difficulty in getting started persists, I would begin to search my mental transference file for the flags I put up during the history taking, to try to determine if there may be transference issues operating at this time that are inhibiting the patient. If I have not already done so, I would ask: "How did you feel about our last session?" Or, "How did you feel after you left here last time?" If this is not productive, I might ask how the patient felt coming here today—anxious, blah? Or, "Did you think about the upcoming session during the week?" Or, "How did you feel/what were your thoughts sitting in the waiting room?" Or, "How did you feel talking to a psychologist/psychiatrist, man/woman," moving in slightly closer to the possible transference. I would *not* ask in the beginning: "How did you feel talking to me? Did you have any feelings about me after you left?" This is too threatening in the early stages of therapy, while the patient does not know what is expected, and will still be behaving as if they are in a social situation. The patient will politely answer that everything about you and talking to you was just fine, and since you will be unable to explore it further, you will unknowingly be reinforcing this type of response to transferentially loaded questions.

In describing the flow of the middle phase of therapy in this chapter, I will necessarily refer to concepts that have already been introduced in earlier chapters. They will be expanded upon here, with examples. The reader may find it helpful to refer back to the earlier chapters if he or she does not feel familiar enough with the concepts.

What happens in therapy after the history taking can be amazing. Your patient starts to adjust to the feeling of being held in a safe place where anything can be said, and where someone is genuinely interested in what the person has to say. For some patients, putting their toes in the water first and slowly going in deeper feels better than diving in with an explosion of affect or a cathartic telling of painful events. Some patients feel guarded at first; some, especially those who have had prior experience of any kind of empathic relationship, sense right away that the therapist is on their side and that they now have support. These latter patients may feel incredibly relieved, and may show this by crying or becoming emotional in some other way.

As was mentioned in chapter 2, *listening* empathically to your patient may not be as easy as it sounds. Freud described the listening posture of the psychoanalyst as evenly suspended, evenly hovering, free-floating attention (Freud, 1912b). Empathic listening is especially important in the beginning of therapy so that you can get a good understanding of your patient and so that you can give a clear indication to him or her that you do grasp the meaning of what they are saying. Remember that what you are attempting to facilitate is the formation of a warm working alliance and the experience for your patient of being deeply understood. Once this process has been undertaken through a great deal of hard work on the part of both patient and therapist, then it is much easier to proceed with pointing out contradictions to the patient or offering interpretations. Do not assume that an *alliance* has been formed because your patient smiles at you or agrees with you; this may just as well indicate a resistance to treatment. The alliance does not come easily, and as was mentioned in chapter 1, should not be expected to occur within the first few weeks or even months.

Some time ago, I was referred two young female patients who were students at the same private high school, where the suicide of one of their companions, a 17-year-old woman in her final year, had occurred. Despite the fact that the patients were a year apart and had both come for the same presenting reason, which was their parents' concern about how they were reacting to the suicide and worry about their own emotional stability, they reacted in very different ways to the experience of being in treatment. Ms. E, who was a close friend of the woman who had died, was herself in her final year and having considerable problems continuing with her studies. Her parents had been separated for about two years and she lived alone with her mother in an apartment, fairly far from the school. Her relationship with her mother was quite close; she was able to share with her a lot of her feelings about social difficulties at school and about the suicide. When she told her mother that she was spending a fair amount of her studying time "talking" to her dead friend, her mother thought it best that she come for help. After only one or two missed appointments, Ms. E settled into her therapy fairly quickly and seemed relieved to have someone outside of home or school to talk to. Although part of her social difficulties at school revolved around her feeling different from the other students, because she lived in an apartment and had parents who were separated, she did not seem to mind this additional difference of having to see a psychologist. The probability of her developing an alliance with me had seemed high at the beginning of her treatment as her close and rewarding relationships with her mother and her friend's mother and sister would probably have predisposed her toward the expectation of having another positive relationship with an older female. As she began to be able to express her grief over the loss of her close friend and to see how her feelings in this event were similar to her feelings about the loss of her father from the home, she began to relax a little more at school. She met with her guidance counsellor to draw up a reasonable program of study, which she was able to follow. She also allowed herself to maintain a close connection with her late friend's family, particularly her mother and sister, whom she had feared losing as well. All of these gains,

THE ONGOING THERAPY

and Ms. E's willingness to continue exploring her thoughts and feelings, were evidence that an alliance had developed. At the end of our rather brief six months together, Ms. E informed me that she had gotten accepted to university and that she had decided what she wanted to study—psychology. She promised to write me a card from school.

Ms. F, on the other hand, who was seen for approximately the same length of time in treatment, never developed a working alliance. This 16-year-old woman, who was also a friend of the suicide victim, although not as close a friend, was the youngest child in a family of three siblings, and was the only child left living at home with her mother and stepfather. Her older brother had left home for university, and her older sister, who had been hospitalized for psychiatric problems, was traveling around to various cities and living in different relationships, unable to settle. Ms. F seemed most attached to this sister, and was quite certain that she was exactly like her underneath the front she chose to show to the world, that is, possibly psychotic. This young woman drove herself hard in school and did not allow herself to have much fun, her only recreation being an involvement in acting in school plays, which seemed to reinforce her habit of hiding her real self from others. She often put herself into situations with older students and then tried to compete with them. In therapy, she talked quite a lot about her older sister's problems and was never able to be totally unguarded about herself. She denied having difficulty in handling the loss of her friend through suicide. Although she seemed very vulnerable, she could not let herself trust me enough to help her with her bad feelings about herself and her fear that she might be like her sister. She ended treatment early by telephoning to cancel her last two sessions.

In terms of how you as a therapist will react to your patient and to the material that he or she brings, what you will learn about yourself eventually, if you keep an eye on yourself while you are working, is: (1) what ways of listening help you to understand exactly what your patient is saying and (2) what techniques help to "protect" you from getting swallowed up in the intensity of your patient's emotions. Many therapists find that regarding the patient and his or her problems as a puzzle that has to be solved is helpful to them; this is basically a use of intellectualization. As discussed in the section on empathy in chapter 1, it is imperative that some form of cognitive activity be happening in the therapist interlaced with the affective, empathic endeavor. I find that thinking theoretically, in particular psychodynamically, in an ongoing way throughout the session, helps me to pull away from the emotional quagmire. It enables me to indulge my fascination for figuring out why my patient is expressing these feelings at this time and how they connect either to what has been said in past sessions or to what is going on currently in the here-and-now, in terms of my patient's personality, their difficulties in life, and the transference to me. Of course there are times when less thinking and more pure feeling with the patient is happening in the therapist. If you stay completely in your head and do not let yourself experience the emotions—particularly the feelings of rage or sadness—that your patient describes, then you will be unable to be empathic. If you stay completely on a feeling level, then you will be unable to help your patient understand their feelings in the context of their personality structure and will not be offering them any more than a good friend may offer. For example, in the case of Ms. E, described above, during one session she broke down and sobbed about losing her friend. Even though intellectually I was aware that some of the intensity of her emotion could be accounted for by her feelings of loss over her father leaving the home, which she had never mourned, and some by her feelings of guilt over not being a good enough friend to the suicide victim, I

THE ONGOING THERAPY

stayed with her on a feeling level for a long time trying to feel the extent of the pain she was experiencing. I only offered her my intellectual thoughts after I was certain she had had enough time with her emotions. This requires from the therapist: (1) the ability to empathize; (2) the ability to think at the same time (eg., about the loss of the father and the relationship with the lost friend); (3) the judgment to decide on which type of intervention is most helpful and most therapeutic for the patient. The process for the therapist sometimes feels like a movement "up" and "down," up to a cognitive level and down to an emotional level at different times during the session, usually not staying in any one place for the entire session. If someone has just suffered a loss, the death of someone close, or has just been involved in a crisis, remaining on a feeling level for the entire session, or even many sessions, may well be justified.

The delicate balance between emotions and cognition that is required comes from the experience of seeing a variety of patients, learning how to formulate hypotheses, getting to know how certain issues affect you as a therapist, and also what types of patients you find it easier to feel empathy toward and which ones seem more difficult for you to understand. Many students have found it surprising to discover how strenuous it is to spend an hour with a patient in psychotherapy. They have not previously realized the enormous amount of cognitive work that is going on behind the scenes, as it were, in the therapist's head, while the patient is talking. It is important to be able to keep several hypotheses about what might be happening with your patient floating around in your head so that, at the appropriate time, you can select the one that seems most likely and try it out with him or her. If it is rejected by your patient the first time it is presented, do not discard it completely, but try to make a decision as to which mental "file" it should go into. Should it be tried again at a later time or should it be modified in some way and perhaps tried again right away? If you can keep it stored away, you will have it still floating in your mind for when you need to select it again. Staying loose mentally should produce the most therapeutic results. You need to remain open to hearing what your patient is saying, no matter what impression you have already formed, and be able to keep several hypotheses on your mental screen, moving back and forth from one to another, kind of like intellectual rocking.

Greenson (1967) describes his mental processes in an instance when he had difficulty understanding one of his patients as follows:

> At this point I change the way I am listening to her. I shift from listening from the outside to listening from the inside. I have to let a part of me become the patient, and I have to go through her experiences as if I were the patient and to introspect what is going on in me as they occur. What I am trying to describe are the processes that occur when one empathizes with a patient. I let myself experience the different events the patient has described and I also let myself experience the analytic hour, her associations and her affects as she seems to have gone through them in the hour. I go back over the patient's utterances and transform her words into pictures and feelings in accordance with her personality. I let myself associate to these pictures with *her* life experiences, *her* memories, *her* fantasies. As I have worked with this patient over the years I have built up a working model of the patient consisting of her physical appearance, her behavior, her ways of moving, her desires, feelings, defenses, values, attitudes, etc. It is this working model of the patient that I shift into the foreground as I try to capture what she was experiencing. The rest of me is deemphasized and isolated for the time being [pp. 367–368].

Mr. G, a 39-year-old single businessman, came to see me for psychotherapy to understand his problems in relationships with women. He had been intimately involved with several women in the previous few years, all of whom presumably had wanted to marry him, but to none of whom he could make a commitment. Some of his relationships were with friends of his former girl friends, which had complicated things further. At the time of entering treatment, he was involved with a 28-year-old woman who had never had a long-term relationship before. When he again came up against his old pattern of wanting to leave, she suggested that he get professional help and he complied.

In his first session, Mr. G seemed anxious to impress me with his business success and had a great deal of difficulty in talking about the more personal areas of his life. He did manage to tell me that his mother, a domineering woman, did not think of him as having "made it" in the world, because he had never completed university. At the end of the session, he assured me that he wanted to work on his problems in making commitments and in particular, in relation to the woman he was currently seeing. Mr. G arrived at our second session one week later with a smile on his face and announced that he was engaged. He had thought about things after our talk and apparently decided there was no reason to delay any longer. He had subsequently bought his female friend, now a zealous believer in the power of psychologists, a large diamond ring.

As Mr. G's therapist, I was obviously at a decision point. I asked my patient to tell me a little more about his thoughts and feelings leading up to the engagement. While listening to him, I silently hypothesized that the engagement was a form of acting out, and that the first session must have been so extremely anxiety-provoking for him that he had needed to call on this defensive form of behavior. I thought about whether it was the *content* of what he had talked about. Being in psychotherapy might lead to his finding out information about himself that he had fended off knowing, and that this time he was really on the hook and would have to examine his difficulty with commitment. This might lead to having to make the commitment which he feared so much, and so he had perversely decided to do it and get it over with. On the other hand, it might be the *transference*, the only clue for which I had seen so far being in his description of his mother whose expectations he could not meet, in which case I may have already been perceived by him in the first session as this critical mother. His smile and excitement over the news could also have been an indication that he thought he had done something right, and that I would be pleased. Thinking that it was probably some combination of the above, my next decision was what to *do* about this. I decided to store my thoughts for the time being and *not* to give the patient an interpretation of the acting out at this time for the following reasons: (1) I did not know the patient well enough to know if any of my hypotheses might be true; (2) because it was so early in treatment and there was no working alliance as yet, I did not know how he would react to hearing my thoughts and I feared I might lose the patient in the way his mother had, by "criticizing" him with an observation or an interpretation; (3) an interpretation might prematurely curtail the patient's own further exploration of his thoughts and feelings about the engagement and perhaps whatever insights that might grow out of this exploration; (4) I wanted my patient to learn that insights in therapy will be gained by the slow and thoughtful work of a partnership, not by my giving him explanations of his behavior.

The only reasons I could think of for pointing out the acting out were: (1) to save the patient and his fiancée some embarrassment by their possibly calling off the engagement before announcing it further; or (2) to show my patient how clever I was to have spotted this (rather obvious) piece of defensive behavior. Therefore I encouraged Mr. G to spend this second session telling me his conscious thoughts about being engaged. Near the end of the session, he spontaneously began to talk about his mother again and his ambivalence about telephoning her with the news, which gave me a little more data to support the transference part of the hypothesis.

In this case, then, for the next few sessions, I worked at getting to know my patient, trying to understand him and to empathize with him. I spent a fair amount of time on a feeling level with him, helping him to help me get a sense of his world, and in the process, legitimizing the emotional part of him. After about six months of therapy, he asked me what I thought about his engagement. This was a signal to me that he was ready to explore the issue himself, and we did so for the next several weeks. By the time my suggestion about his possible acting out was offered, I knew a great deal more about his relationship with his mother and was able to predict more accurately the effect that this interpretation would have on him. He was by then more aware of the intensity of his feelings about having tried unsuccessfully all of his life to please his mother, and was able to begin to accept that he might have a reaction to feeling that he had not pleased me. After this point, Mr. G stayed in treatment for two years, deciding that he would stay engaged but postpone the wedding. He was able to work through his rage at his mother and to become conscious of his defending against an identification with his inadequate father. He changed jobs to one with slightly less pressure and status, but which he enjoyed more, and after the two years, he felt readier to take the plunge into marriage.

It is difficult to separate the process of psychodynamic psychotherapy from the process of *interpretation*; in fact, it is almost impossible to discuss one without the other since interpretation is an intricate part of the therapist's function. By offering an interpretation to the patient, the therapist is offering a dynamic understanding of a patient's thoughts, feelings, behaviors or dreams, to help the patient put these into a context. Chapter 1 gives a fairly detailed definition of the technique of interpretation. Because interpretations can address themselves to almost every area of therapy and, indeed of life, it is sometimes difficult to determine exactly how and when they should be used. In general, an interpretation will be most successful if it has been well thought through by the therapist, if it is correctly timed in terms of being said when the patient is readiest to hear it, and if a working alliance exists between the patient and the therapist. As was stated earlier, interpretations often have to be given more than once to be able to be heard and reflected on by the patient.

Sometimes an interpretation can change the flow of the therapy, as the patient suddenly becomes aware of what he or she has been thinking or doing. Often interpretations are used to help the patient see how he or she has been *resisting* treatment, as explained in chapter 1 under the heading of resistance, where several examples of resistance are given. When you are interpreting a resistance, you are pointing out the patient's (usually) unconscious motivation to obstruct the therapy, and helping the patient to analyze why he or she might be doing this at this time. The hope is that this type of comment will not only give the patient valuable insight into his or her actions but will assist the person in changing behavior enough to be able to move along in treatment. Referring to the example of Mr. G, above, his acting out by getting engaged could have been interpreted as a resistance to treatment. In his own mind, he might have been closing off the exploratory process by "solving" his problems with commitment before his therapy had even begun. However, as timing in giving an interpretation is of extreme importance, it was decided in this case that the resistance could better be dealt with by providing a safer climate for the patient before offering an interpretation. It is helpful to remember that most patients will experience an interpretation as criticism in the beginning of treatment. This is because the greater part of the population grew up with parents who gave them criticisms, not nonjudgmental observations or interpretations of their behavior. The patient has to learn to see the interpretation as a helpful

THE ONGOING THERAPY

observation and as the type of thinking they can do about their own behavior as well, the purpose being to facilitate their treatment or to change a maladaptive behavior pattern so that they will be more satisfied with their lives. If given in the second session, the interpretation that Mr. G might have been trying to please me as he had so often tried to please his mother, and had committed exactly the action that would *dis*please me as he may have done unconsciously with her, would have had an entirely different effect on the therapy. After six months, the effect it had was to cause Mr. G to change his wedding plans, a reasonable action which allowed him to work in therapy on his underlying difficulties.

Silences are sometimes resistances, and because they are particularly difficult for student therapists to handle, an elaboration on the understanding of silences and the technique for using them productively is in order here. Most people feel uncomfortable with silences and, particularly in social situations, try to fill them with chatter as quickly as possible. The student who has been involved in group psychotherapy will have seen in that milieu quite clearly how different individuals react to silences in different ways. For some it is extremely stressful or embarrassing; some patients feel it is their "fault"; others feel quite comfortable and safe when there is silence. Silence in psychotherapy always provides grist for the mill, often, as mentioned above, for the resistance mill.

Before attempting to understand your patient's silences, or, perhaps more realistically, after your first experience of prolonged silence in a session, it will be important to examine in supervision your own reaction to silences, both in everyday situations and in psychotherapy, so that you will be able to predict the effect a patient's silence will have on you. For example, how do you feel as a therapist during a silence; how much silence can you tolerate comfortably; and what, if anything, about silence

THE ONGOING THERAPY

bothers you? Beginning therapists often have trouble tolerating long silences, that is, a silence of more than two or three minutes, feeling the need to rush in and discover what the patient is thinking, or possibly feeling a sense of failure because their patient is no longer speaking to them or sharing their thoughts with them. Interns and others may also experience the feeling of being excluded during silences, which may relate to previous experiences in family or social situations. One of my students thought I was being unnecessarily hard on her and her patient by asking her to wait longer during periods of silence; she defended herself by saying it was cruel to let her patient "sit there and stew." If you find silences unbearable, this should be discussed in supervision and a plan for dealing with them decided upon.

When a patient is silent, it usually indicates that a censoring or resistance process is in operation, which may be conscious or unconscious. What the patient has just been saying may have triggered another thought, but not a thought that is easy to share. The patient may actually be aware of what he or she is thinking about, but may not dare say it out loud. Or the patient may only be aware of thinking about "nothing," having a "blank mind," and may not be conscious of what is being repressed. Some patients need silence to reflect on what they or you have just said or on how they are feeling. They may be feeling something they have never felt before. These patients need the space of the silence to gather their thoughts before continuing. In any case, it is important to allow the patient to have the experience of silence, without feeling that this is wrong; therefore, the therapist should be able to allow a certain amount of time to elapse comfortably.

You will never know about the conscious or unconscious processes that are going on in your patient during the silence if you break a silence with your own agenda, or with what you imagine is troubling your patient. Usually the best first course of action in dealing with a silence is to let the patient be the one to break it. This means that you have to be patient and calm and be able to continue holding him or her in a safe way during the silence. The patient will eventually feel like telling you what is on their mind. It is helpful to observe the patient for nonverbal cues such as avoidance of eye contact, blushing, scratching, and so on. For most patients, when they are thinking during a silence, they will be looking at the floor or elsewhere and when they have finished their thought they will then be able to look directly at you, signaling that they are ready for contact again. If this occurs, then it is usually best not to interrupt while they are looking away and thinking. If the silence goes on for an inordinate period of time and in your clinical judgment is unproductive, then you can break in, but always by trying to understand what was happening with the patient during this time. It is important not to be critical about silences or to make an intervention that causes the patient to feel that silences cannot be tolerated in treatment. Comments such as: "I'm wondering what you're thinking about right now"; or, "Can you tell me how you're feeling right now"; or, "Are you having any thoughts that you could try to share with me," all focus on the patient's experience and allow for the possibility that the therapist may be surprised at hearing what the patient has been thinking about. Once the patient volunteers the information, it is always interesting to explore what it was about that particular thought, feeling, or topic that made the patient go silent.

Sometimes silences will occur in patterns, that is, patients may always become silent when certain topics are raised or at certain points in the session, especially right at the beginning, or near the end. An observation about this is often helpful so that the patient can explore what it is about those topics or about beginning or ending sessions that produces these effects. There are patients, of course, who are never silent, and patients who, if not prompted, could be silent through most of the session. In terms of the former, the volume of speech and lack of reflection may constitute a resistance and should be commented on by the therapist at the appropriate time. When patients seem more comfortable in total silence, this may indicate a fear of the therapist or the therapy situation, rage at having to be in therapy, or a social style that indicates severe shyness with others. Again, this should be explored with the patient.

There are certain exciting moments in the course of the therapy when illuminating glimpses into the patient's unconscious can occur. Often patients in psychodynamic psychotherapy will *free associate*, whether or not they are lying on a couch. This occurs when a patient describes the exact thought that came to mind at a specific moment in association to another thought or event. The patient's spontaneity and tone of voice tip off the therapist to the genuineness of the free association. Also, often the thought appears to be a *non sequitur*, particularly to the patient, but the reason for its coming to mind can usually be determined fairly easily and gives a great deal of information. A free association will often be introduced by the patient with the words: "I don't know why I'm thinking this but . . ."; or, "It seems ridiculous but this thought just came into my mind—it doesn't relate to anything I've been saying."

One of my patients, a 45-year-old married social worker who was heading toward the termination of a relatively long-term psychotherapy, had for several weeks preceding the ending been experiencing an unusual amount of anxiety about it which she could not readily identify. She started one session by mentioning her ending date and then stated that there was a tune that kept playing in her head. She hummed a little: It turned out to be *She's Leaving Home*, a Beatles' song that speaks sadly from the perspective of the parents of a young woman leaving home.

From this association, she was able to elaborate on her fear that I did not really want her to terminate and would miss her too much, as her mother had, the latter having become seriously ill when she had gotten married. Clearly her ending with me was reminiscent of that earlier separation and she needed to know that I did not need her in the way her mother apparently did and that I would survive her going. This "new" material, that is, her concern for *my* wellbeing, emerged as a result of her free association.

Dreams are, of course, another window into the patient's unconscious that can provide valuable material and possibly insights of which the patient may have been previously unaware. When Freud wrote *The Interpretation of Dreams*, published in 1900, he had apparently begun to see that understanding the structure and meaning of a patient's dreams increased his skill of interpretation in the treatment. As a result of this, he was able to rely more and more on the patient's spontaneous production of material. In the first chapter of *The Interpretation of Dreams*, Freud quotes a beautiful description of dreaming written by an earlier German author, Hildebrandt:

> There are few of us who could not affirm, from our own experience, that there emerges from time to time in the creations and fabrics of the genius of dreams a depth and intimacy of emotion, a tenderness of feeling, a clarity of vision, a subtlety of observation, and a brilliance of wit such as we should never claim to have at our permanent command in our waking lives. There lies in dreams a marvellous poetry, an apt allegory, an incomparable humour, a rare irony. A dream looks upon the world in a light of strange idealism and often enhances the effects of what it sees by its deep understanding of their essential nature. It pictures earthly beauty to our eyes in a truly heavenly splendour and clothes dignity with the highest majesty, it shows us our everyday fears in the ghastliest shape and turns our amusement into jokes of indescribable pungency. And sometimes, when we are awake and still under the full impact of an experience like one of these,

we cannot but feel that never in our lives has the real world offered us its equal [cited in Freud, 1900, pp. 62–63].

"The interpretation of dreams is the royal road to a knowledge of the unconscious activities of the mind" (p. 608), Freud wrote in 1900, and since then dreams have become an important part of psychoanalytic and psychodynamic psychotherapy content. Freud's concepts can provide a useful basis for beginning to understand a dream. For example, the manifest content of the dream (the surface story), latent content (the underlying motivation for the dream and the symbolic meaning of the story), and day's residue (the triggering factor from the patient's waking life, usually in the day preceding the dream, that precipitated the dream or that trails off into the dream and starts the story), are still utilized in more modern psychoanalytically oriented treatment, at least conceptually, by therapists. There is a danger lurking here, and that is why this book does not elaborate on ways of interpreting dreams; that is, for the student of psychodynamic therapy it is essential to realize that this is *the patient's* dream, and therefore it is *the patient's* thoughts and associations about the dream that are of the essence here. Laying on an "interpretation" of the dream shortly after hearing it at best sounds like crystal-ball gazing and at worst stops your patient from working with the dream if he or she is so inclined and leads to incorrect expectations of the therapist.

As productions of the patient, dreams are precious material and should be treated with care. However, if it is too evident to your patient that you value his or her dreams, they may reward you by bringing too much dream material to the sessions, or may start dreaming just for you. In most cases, though, when your patient begins to tell you a dream, it is important to listen to all the details carefully and not to interrupt. Because of the nature of dream material, patients will often be embarrassed by the content of the dream or by the lack of a coherent story.

THE ONGOING THERAPY

Encourage them to go on and tell the dream just as they remember it, disregarding logic, even if it is only a piece of the dream that they remember. Some therapists like to repeat to the patient what they have heard once the dream has been related, to be certain that they have heard all of it. Then you are ready to begin examining your patient's associations to the dream.

When I was an intern, I had a patient, a 27-year-old woman, who presented me with a dream very early in treatment. In the dream, she was in my office seated at a table eating vegetable soup. The soup was filled with all kinds of hearty chunky pieces of green vegetables. She was eating rather slowly until I came and sat down beside her, at which point she began spooning the soup into her mouth as quickly as she could. The dream ended with her being unable to finish the soup.

Despite the ending of the dream, my immediate association to it was that this patient was experiencing me as a wonderfully nurturing person, giving her the most nutritious of food, and that her increased speed in eating when I came along showed her willingness to cooperate in the treatment with me. Fortunately, I was able to keep my thoughts to myself and to allow my patient to tell me her associations to the dream. She said it had called up for her the image of a very domineering aunt, a woman who told everyone in her family, particularly her mother, what to do. As a young child, this patient had rebelled against her mother by not eating, and it so troubled the mother that she occasionally invited the aunt over at lunchtime to "get me to eat." Apparently, this aunt would sit beside my patient at the table, exhorting her to "chew, chew; swallow!" with every bite, which, of course, had been a rather terrible experience for her. So much for student narcissism. Needless to say, this led to a revealing discussion of my patient's feelings of being in psychotherapy and to her experience of me as moving her along faster than she wished.

When working with a dream, then, it is usually best to start with what stands out most in the dream *for the patient.* Often the patient will tell this by repeating something over and over or by being mystified over one particular part of the dream that does not seem to fit. If not, I might start off the exploration by asking: "What part of your dream seems most compelling to you?" These pieces can then be explored with the patient, asking for his or her associations to each part, step by step. Students in psychology who have used the Rorschach may find it helpful at times to think of the parts of the dream as analogous to inkblots; however, it is possible to become overly obsessional about this and to lose sight of the dream as a whole. If the patient is truly stuck and if you have an association that comes from your unconscious that you feel is emerging from your empathy with your patient, it is sometimes appropriate to offer it to the patient. You need to make it clear, however, that this is something that has come to your mind but that may not feel right to the patient. Sometimes patients will modify your comments to suit themselves and this will trigger new thoughts and associations for them. However, it must be emphasized here that this is tricky territory and that the therapist must be aware of whether the patient accepts or rejects their comments due to a transference issue or to resistance, and so on. Incidentally, I find that my unconscious associations to my patients' dream material are just as important as any interpretation I might make and often provide me with transferential or countertransferential insights, whether or not I share them with the patient.

Dreams may describe in different ways how worried the patient is about some issue or other, how stuck in treatment, or alternatively how much progress has been made, sometimes before that progress has been consolidated in the person's conscious life. An example of the latter is found in a dream that Mr. G, the patient who got engaged after his first session, described near the end of his treatment with me. As our work

THE ONGOING THERAPY

together had progressed, Mr. G had talked about problems he had experienced with sexuality, particularly an embarrassment that his penis was too small, since his older brother had ridiculed him about the size of his penis when they were younger. He also had problems with premature ejaculation, which had been an ongoing difficulty in his relationships and which was starting to improve, as the causes for it were explored dynamically. The dream was as follows:

Mr. G was in a tunnel where there were many sets of train tracks. He was driving a train and saw a "little train" go by. The little train was painted with very bright, primary colors. But he was in control of the bigger train. He wasn't sure if he could steer the train and, indeed, the train went off the track. He felt frustrated by this, but managed to get the train back on the track and to continue driving it, while the little train remained stopped.

When I asked for his associations to the dream, Mr. G laughed and said there was so much going in and out of tunnels that he thought he should have needed a cigarette after waking up! He stated that he thought the little train, so brightly colored, was a child's train and represented a little penis, like the one he had had in childhood. He was pleased as he told me that that train had been on the sidelines; he wasn't in it. He was glad to have been in control of the larger train, even though it had gone off the track, which he spontaneously connected to his problems with premature ejaculation. He then said: "Well, I must be farther along at mastering this problem than I thought, because in the dream, I got back on track and felt very powerful."

Most dreams that are brought into treatment are used as forms of communication by the patient in several ways, and it is often productive to pursue what the patient was trying to tell the therapist by bringing this dream at this time. As well, the patient may have modified the dream for presentation to the therapist, that is, in the intervening time between waking up and the session hour. This modification process is sometimes conscious and sometimes not, and may be able to be discovered after the patient has had time to talk about the dream in the therapy. Some patients can only talk about certain parts of their life (e.g., their sexual activities or fantasies) by couching them in the more acceptable manner of their having appeared in a dream. Some may be able to describe their anger toward or fear of their therapist only by having a dream that relates to this when analyzed. For some patients the dream is a gift to the therapist; they are saying, "See how much I believe in our work together and, in particular, in your orientation to it—I have brought you a marvellous dream." For others, not remembering dreams can be a resistance: "I had a dream last night that was pretty heavy, and I think you were in it, but I can't remember it."

Before leaving this discussion of dreams, it must be stated that not every dream needs to be completely understood or even closely examined. It may be that some dreams seem more significant for the patient or appear at a particular turning-point in the treatment; other dreams may seem more "ordinary" or may lead to dead-ends when explored in a meticulous manner. Sometimes one of the latter types of dreams, while not seeming important at the time it was dreamt, will suddenly be recalled by the patient in a later session, and is able to be better understood in retrospect. Even though dreams may fascinate or interest you, then, do not force your patient into analyzing every dream. As in all parts of psychotherapy, working with patients in uncovering the possible underlying meaning of their dreams must be done with empathy and sensitivity.

As therapy progresses, new issues that were not brought out in the initial sessions will undoubtedly arise. In the case of Ms. C, mentioned in chapter 3, for example, who presented initially

THE ONGOING THERAPY

with memory problems, it was discovered several months into treatment that she had been sexually molested by her father. In her case, her father was the only one in the family who had shown her any love and acceptance and so it was extremely difficult for her to "remember" the sexual activity earlier in her therapy. She was afraid that this knowledge would affect both her feelings for, and her therapist's impression of, this father whom she had needed so desperately in her childhood. Mr. G could not have revealed sensitive sexual information to me while I was being perceived by him as a critical mother, and this material emerged only after he felt safe enough with me. Painful and embarrassing material of this nature is usually not revealed in the earlier sessions and sometimes may not even be disclosed until very close to termination (see chapter 6). When new material does emerge, it can be carefully explored with the patient and often the reasons for its not having emerged earlier can be explored as well.

Another phenomenon that occurs almost imperceptibly as the therapy moves along is that the therapist will hear the same material from the history or earlier sessions again, but now it sounds different, taking on a deeper meaning once the patient is better known. When Mr. G related in the history that he could never please a critical and domineering mother, this did not affect me as much as when he raised it again, one year later, in the context of his sexual problems. At that point, it was not a stranger who was being harassed by his mother, but *my* Mr. G, and this caused my reaction to the same material to be quite different.

FLAGGING THE TRANSFERENCE IN THE ONGOING THERAPY

Even while the therapeutic relationship is in an embryonic state, there will already be issues regarding the patient's experience of the therapy which will continue in some manner as themes throughout the treatment. As was mentioned in the section on transference in chapter 1, these issues are displacements of the patient's perceptions of significant others from their past onto the therapist, and they can also sometimes be projections of the patient's own feelings into the therapy situation. Through these early themes, one gets a sense of how the patient is mentally categorizing the psychotherapy, and how it is being labeled. They will, of course, use situations as well as people from earlier times as "labels" from which they can choose to help them deal with the novelty of the psychotherapeutic environment and relationship. Discovering the projections and displacements is an ongoing task for the therapist; once you are aware of them, then you can flag them and make a judgment about whether, and/or when, to help your patient become aware of them by giving an interpretation. However, it should be borne in mind that there is no transference reaction, no matter how fantastic, without a germ of truth, and there is no realistic relationship without some trace of a transference fantasy. All patients in psychoanalytically oriented therapy have realistic and objective perceptions of, and reactions to, their therapist, alongside of their transference reactions and their working alliance (Greenson, 1967).

It is impossible to overestimate the impact that the personal figure of the therapist has on the patient. Everything that you do and say takes on the utmost importance for them. Although a transference is developing, your patient will be extremely sensitive to any real clues about your personality that you give off. Any comments that patients make about you must be explored and understood, so that the "real" elements can be sifted out from the transferential ones. As has been mentioned earlier, the most probable transferences to emerge throughout most of the treatment are mother/father transferences. By the middle of treatment, sibling transferences can also be manifested.

There are several ways of identifying transference reactions: (1) the patient has an excessive reaction to a statement or event in the therapy, or possibly an underreaction (e.g., no affective reaction when you would naturally expect one); (2) there is a change in behavior not usual for the patient (e.g., lateness, coming early, talking less or more than usual, more seductive or flirtatious than usual); (3) the patient suddenly starts dressing up, or dressing down, for the session; (4) the patient expresses a greater than usual interest in the therapist's life outside the office; (5) the patient brings a gift; (6) the patient stays around the hallway or the office building for an excessively long period of time after the session is over. These are some of the more frequently seen manifestations of transference, and suggested ways of dealing with them follow.

The therapist's response to these indications of transference is critical. What is of utmost importance to remember, as has been mentioned earlier, is that you are dealing with a *transference*, and that this relates to the *patient's* history and probably only has a "germ of truth" that relates to you as a person. As exhilarating as an idealizing transference feels to the therapist, as demoralizing as a devaluing, negative transference feels, and as uncomfortable as an erotic transference feels, try to keep in mind that these feelings are being *displaced* from people in the patient's past onto you, and are almost always able to be understood in this light. If you stay with your patient, always listening to what they are saying, and trying to grasp the world from their point of view, you will be able, piece by piece, to unravel the meaning of the various transference reactions that will emerge during the course of the therapy.

The displacements from the past are, however, often triggered by elements in the present therapist–patient relationship. Thus there are two "levels" of transference operating simultaneously: the part of the therapist–patient relationship that is "real" and precipitates the arousal of feelings from the past, and the transference reaction that represents quite clearly in itself the displacement from the patient's past important figures. Sometimes it is difficult for the therapist to know on which level to start working with the patient, and so it may be helpful to envision it as a two-step process. The first step would be to talk a little about the therapist–patient present-day relationship, including the components in that relationship that are contributing to the patient's current feelings. For example, one might say: "It seems that you are feeling angry at me right now." The observation about what the patient may be feeling has to be made in a nonthreatening way so that the patient can hear it and agree with it if, in fact, it is the case. Once the anger toward the therapist has been established and explored, as it relates to the current situation, the relationship to past figures can be traced. In the above example, let us say that the patient felt angry because he or she felt a session ended too abruptly. The session may have, in reality, ended too soon for the patient, and the therapist, for some reason—either feeling rushed or possibly uncomfortable with having to end the session—may have, in reality, ended it more abruptly than usual. After the patient's feelings about how the session ended have been explored, then any familiar feelings the patient had when this occurred, any memories, can be brought out. For example, the patient might indicate that he or she often felt cut short by mother in the past when trying to discuss important issues. Then the link can be made with the therapist: "When you felt I ended last week's session too abruptly, it reminded you of the feeling that you used to get when your mother cut you off when you were trying to tell her about something that was important to you." In this way the patient can see that (1) they are "allowed" to be angry at the therapist; (2) that the therapist and therapeutic situation survive the anger; (3) that the therapist is, at times, the object of displacement and that *some* of their feelings are not intended for the therapist personally; and (4) that the therapy can stimulate significant feelings from the past that need to be discussed.

THE ONGOING THERAPY

Most transference reactions that are manifested in *changes in behavior* as described above can be dealt with by first making an observation about the behavior. Thus, if the patient is suddenly coming very early or very late, you might start the exploration by saying: "Have you noticed that you've been coming to sessions much earlier/later? Tell me about that." If the patient is being flirtatious, you might comment: "I notice that you're talking to me in a somewhat different manner in the past few sessions; I wonder if you're having any feelings about me that are hard for you to tell me about." If the patient is expressing more than usual interest in your life outside the office, again this must be pointed out and explored. For example: "You've asked me what part of the city I live in. I'm wondering what made you ask me that at this time." Almost never give an answer to questions about you personally (more will be said about this in chapter 7). Instead, after asking about the timing of the thought, I might also ask: "What part of the city do you imagine I live in? Do you have any other thoughts or fantasies about how I live?" In this way, you remain focused *on the patient* and their projections, not on your life; after all, it is what is going on in the patient's mind that is of interest here.

If the patient brings a gift, this is always a difficult situation. Classical psychoanalysts used to be of the opinion that no gifts should ever be accepted from patients and that the meaning of the gift must always be interpreted. More recently, however, the trend has been to accept the gift so as not to risk rejecting the patient, as well as to allow the patient to be able to express certain feelings to the therapist and for him or her to be able to give something to the therapist. However, the motivation for the gift and the patient's fantasies about the gift still must be explored, and oftentimes interpreted. Every therapist must be aware that the gift may not be what it seems on the surface. Many patients bring a gift when they are angry, for instance, as a way of appeasing the therapist, even though the therapist may well be unaware of their anger. Or a gift may be a way of denying their anger or of protecting the therapist from their anger. Some patients bring a gift before they are about to ask a favor of the therapist. Others may be trying to establish that they are the "favorite" of the therapist. A gift can sometimes be a resistance, a trade-off (e.g., "I'll give you this gift if you promise not to pursue talking about my mother's death"). It can also have other meanings in terms of what gifts in general mean to the patient: Who in the patient's past gave them gifts and for what purposes; to whom did they give gifts? Therefore you can first accept the gift graciously, and then ask: "Can you tell me a little about why you thought about giving me this gift now?" Or "Tell me about the meaning of this gift for you." Or, "What were you thinking about when you decided to get me this gift?" Even if it is an "appropriate" gift-giving time, such as Christmas, there is always a story about the particular gift the patient is giving, and most of the time, as long as the discussion is conducted in an accepting and nonjudgmental manner, the patient will appreciate telling it and exploring it.

One of the predictable triggers of transference reactions is *if a patient happens to see you outside of your office*—often a very difficult situation for students. It is highly possible that your patient might at some time see you interacting with others in the hallway, perhaps while the patient is sitting in the waiting room or when they have just left the session. How you interact with people other than them is always very important to the patient. If the other person with whom they see you interact is another patient, this may call up feelings of sibling rivalry (e.g., do you like that patient better, is that patient more interesting?). A patient will assess how you invite the next patient into your office, or how you say good-bye to the patient who precedes them. Therefore, it is always preferable to be as consistent as possible. If you are talking to a colleague in the corridor, while waiting for your patient, perhaps even sharing a joke, more paranoid or sensitive patients may be convinced that you are talking about their case to your colleague, in particular how silly or how difficult their problem is. Sometimes a patient may feel wistfully that this is a part of you they never see, and may even think that you are more energetic or involved in that conversation than you seem to be while passively listening to them. The patient may feel some envy of this and may have fantasies of wishing to be your colleague. There are times, too, when the contrast of your behavior as experienced by the patient outside the session seems grating or unpleasant to them. I once met a patient on the elevator, for example, and I asked someone else to push the floor number. When I asked my patient in the session how she felt about our meeting, she stated that I had been "too aggressive" because of my asking someone else to push the elevator button.

Meeting patients outside the office building in your regular day-to-day life can also stimulate transference feelings for the patient, and sometimes very uncomfortable feelings for the therapist. Some therapists prefer not to acknowledge their patient in these circumstances, rationalizing their own wish not to be seen by saying that it would be embarrassing to the patient to be acknowledged by the therapist in the street. This seems like rudeness to me. If you meet your patient in a restaurant, or at the movies, the best thing to do is to say: Hello. Most patients do not want more than an acknowledgment at these times, and the feeling that you are glad to see them, not that you wish to avoid them. In some situations it is harder to remain gracious than in others, however. I recently met a patient of mine in the lockerroom of the club where I swim regularly, which happens to be located close to my office. I was completely naked, and she was dressed, a rather tricky turn of events. I was able to greet her and to have a *very* brief chat, though I was certainly not at ease! When I asked in our next session how she felt about seeing me there, she said she thought it was "neat" because she was always "baring her soul to me," implying that in that situation I had been baring my body to her. It also emerged that she had been unable to think about me as having an existence outside of my office until that time. This had been a defensive maneuver to counteract the feelings of closeness and dependency she was experiencing. As in all situations in which you are suspicious of potential transference feelings, you *must* ask about the patient's reaction to the encounter outside the session. If you do not ask, your patient will probably not volunteer the information and the opportunity will be lost.

Another extremely important trigger of transference reactions is any *separation* or *vacation*, even if these have been planned well in advance. Unless you have had the experience of being in psychotherapy or psychoanalysis yourself, you will probably underestimate the effect of separations on your patient. There can be difficulties with a long weekend that is a predictable statutory holiday when the patient is also going away, especially if the session falls on a Monday or Friday, even though you may offer an alternate time. It gets much more difficult, of course, if the separation is because of a holiday that you are taking while your patient is staying behind. Separations are generally experienced as some form of abandonment and how patients deal with a separation from you gives a great deal of information about their reactions to loss. This does not mean, of course, that you should never take a holiday. I have supervised students who have wanted to go out of their way to see their patients on Christmas Day or other holidays. As was stated in the section in chapter 1 on the therapist's part in developing the working alliance, it is important that you be as consistent as possible in being there for your patient, and so, of course, you would make every effort not to take unplanned time off. However, there will be occasions when you will want to take time off, or a holiday will fall on the day of a regular session. Not taking any holiday time, or coming to the office on a statutory holiday, may give your patient the message that either you feel they are in such bad shape that they cannot even make it through one or two extra days without you, or that you need to see them for your own sake. They may think you will miss them, you are attracted to them, they are more delightful for you to be with than your family or friends, all of which are unhealthy messages to the patient and certainly poor role-modeling in terms of how holidays should be taken.

You communicate that you honor your contract of treating the session as an extremely important commitment by warning your patient *as far in advance* of an upcoming break as is reasonable. Reasonable notice may differ slightly from patient to patient, some of whom need a great deal of time to discuss their feelings about a break. Bear in mind, however, that because breaks are often painful, too much advance notice may cause the patient to "forget" the upcoming break, having decided at the time of the announcement that there is plenty of time to work on it. Sometimes this is colluded with by the therapist who is feeling guilty about taking the break. The amount of notice given also depends to some extent on the length of time of the treatment. As a general rule, it is best to give about two months' notice of a two- to three-week holiday break.

Similarly, if you see that a statutory holiday is going to fall on a session day, then about one month in advance you should offer your patient an alternate time, if this is at all possible. This tells your patient that: (1) you are looking out for breaks in the treatment; (2) that you respect the commitment and want to try to reschedule if possible; and (3) that you respect their schedule outside of therapy and want to give them as much notice as possible so that they can work out a time to see you. If you are able to see your patient in long-term treatment, for example, for more than one year, then longer notice of two- to three-week breaks can be given. Sometimes patients like to have the opportunity to schedule their own holidays at the same time as yours so that they will not miss too many sessions; in psychoanalysis, this is the norm. It follows, then, that these patients need as much warning as possible because their own family and work life will be affected by their plans for vacation time.

As has been stated, vacations and breaks usually trigger themes of loss for the patient. Often there are feelings of *anger* at your leaving, even though rationally the patient knows that everyone deserves a holiday, and knew the holiday was imminent. There is the feeling of: How can you leave me, especially now. Often it seems as if the break is happening at a particularly bad time in the patient's life, a time when they will be needing you more than ever. Sometimes this is partly based on reality, as at Christmas when many patients see their families and this is very difficult for them; sometimes it is not, but the therapist's leaving precipitates such a feeling of panic that it feels as if there will be a crisis; sometimes a patient will act out by precipitating a crisis so as to try to keep the therapist from going away.

Working with the feelings your patient will have around your break again involves being aware of your own feelings about leaving your patient; this discussion should first be held with your supervisor. Then, bear in mind that your patient will have feelings about it, no matter how much this is denied, that these may not be feelings that either you or your patient enjoy talking about, and that the only way you will know about these feelings is to *ask*. Therefore, once you have announced your intention to take a break, ask your patient: How do you feel about our having to miss two (or more) sessions? The response you get will only be the patient's *first* reaction. As you then proceed with other material in the ensuing sessions, you must keep in mind that the break is coming, and that at least part of how the patient behaves, the material they bring to the session, the dreams they have, may be related to the imminent separation. Therefore, the question of how the patient is feeling about the break must come up again. This is not harping. It gives your patient a chance to tell you more about their reactions to the separation after having an opportunity to think about it. From the history taking, certain transference reactions to breaks may be predictable. Also, what sorts of transferential material has most recently been manifested in the treatment also gives an indication of what to expect. For example, if there is currently a parental transference, your leaving may trigger early experiences of an absent parent, a sick parent, the death of a parent, or a parent who was never there when needed. Your vacation may trigger feelings of being "left out," since you are going away without them, and this may call up a past where parents always excluded the patient from their fun. Or the patient may have fantasies of being the one to go away with you and may feel intense jealousy toward your spouse or whoever they imagine you will be with. If there is a sibling transference, the patient may feel envy that you can take a vacation and they cannot, that you have more money than they do, or are more freed up in some other way.

All of this is, as you can see, very rich material. When these feelings can be evoked, accepted in a nonjudgmental way, and talked about and understood, patients will learn an enormous amount not only about how they react to separation and loss, but about how they are perceiving you at this time. Do not be afraid to ask: "Where do you imagine I am going?" "Who do you imagine I am going away with?" "What do you imagine I am like when away from the office?" "How do you imagine feeling on the first session day of our break?" "What would help you to get through the time with your own family?"

As Basch (1980) has pointed out, the question of whether to actually tell a patient where you are going when you absent yourself from the office cannot be answered with a formula. If you believe that the anxiety of not knowing your whereabouts will serve as a productive stimulus for your patient, it would be incorrect to short-circuit that possibility by giving them the factual information. Basch also states that there may be situations where it would be a depreciation of your patient's capacity for independence to tell them where you will be, and there are patients who would misinterpret such information as indicative of *your* dependence on *them*. For patients in extreme crisis, knowing your general whereabouts may have a calming and settling influence, helping them to understand that you are not totally unavailable to them, and that you will return to them and to their therapy. As treatment progresses, you may want to deal differently with your patient's curiosity about your leaving: just because you may tell the patient your whereabouts one time does not mean that they need to know this on another occasion. Of course the ultimate separation is termination, which will be discussed in the next chapter. How your patient deals with "smaller" separations, such as holidays, will provide a window into how they will deal with the eventual ending of therapy.

In general, then, in the middle phase of the therapy, there will be many new challenges that could not have been entirely predicted from the beginning and history-taking sessions, even by an experienced psychotherapist. There will be brand new material, there will be transference themes, and there will be resistances—sometimes manifested in ingenious ways. You will be challenged as a therapist and as a human being in terms of the maturity of your knowledge and judgment, and your patience and basic ability to care. In terms of your own countertransference, at times it will be extremely difficult to listen to your patient in an empathic way, at times it will be difficult to withhold your own comments and interpretations, to wait for the right time to speak them. At times it will be difficult to understand your own emotions in the session and, once understanding them, to keep them accessible enough to help you understand your patient but contained enough so that they do not interfere with or inhibit your patient's full expression of their emotions. More will be said about the use and management of countertransference in chapters 7 and 8. The task is formidable, but incredibly exciting and rewarding.

6.

Ending

According to Berger (1987), there is no single criterion that is in itself sufficient to demonstrate readiness for termination. He lists, among others, the following indicators that are helpful guidelines in making a judgment with your patient about whether it is time to think about ending: (1) symptomatic improvement; (2) the improved capacity to work and to love; (3) a more comprehensive appreciation of what underlies one's symptoms and conflicts; (4) a greater tolerance for anxiety and depression, and also for pleasure; (5) an improved sense of autonomy; (6) the ability to use newfound insights to adaptively alter day-to-day functioning (pp. 259–260).

The decision to terminate therapy is certainly not always clear-cut. In addition to this, student therapists often encounter specific difficulties with ending, some of which pertain to the circumstances of internship, for example, having to stop treatment early because of the conclusion of an internship placement or residency. Before we consider the process of termination, let us first discuss the importance of an ongoing examination with your supervisor of *your* feelings about ending treatment with your patient. How tolerant, empathic, and accepting you are of your patient's reactions to ending therapy will depend on many factors, some of which may include: (1) your own past personal experiences with endings and losses; (2) your own historical

ENDING

growing up and separation experiences with parents who were or were not able to let go of you at the appropriate time; (3) your own current needs to continue seeing this patient—because of the way the patient makes you feel in treatment, or possibly because of your relationship with your supervisor which may depend on your continuing to see this patient, or for other reasons; (4) your possible guilt over being relieved to "get rid of" this patient; (5) the ending of the therapy coinciding with other endings in your own life (e.g., the ending of an internship or life as a student, or even leaving town, and so on). Several of these factors, particularly numbers 1 and 2, do not need to be discussed in the same depth in supervision as they would be in your own personal therapy. However, it is important to be aware of, and to be able to identify, when these sorts of issues and other feelings about termination may be affecting you. If you do not discuss the reactions that are mobilized in you in enough detail, you will find yourself inhibited by them and unable to be truly empathic to your patient as together you move toward the ending of treatment. As you may have realized by now, each phase of the therapy is mined with triggers for countertransference feelings which, if not explored in supervision and with other colleagues, will detrimentally affect the course of your work with your patient; the phase of termination is certainly no exception.

You may be in the fortunate position of being able to carry on with your patient until the *ending would naturally occur* or of being able to transport your patient with you to your next internship setting. (The latter raises issues of "specialness" for the patient which must be discussed: For example, Am I the only patient you are taking with you? Why are you taking me?) Then, the cue to begin thinking about ending in psychodynamically oriented psychotherapy, sometimes different from other theoretical approaches, usually comes from the patient. However, as the therapist, you should have a sense that some of the goals mentioned at the beginning of this chapter, and that you and your patient have understood as important, have been achieved. Is your patient functioning better in their life, as well as could be expected, and has your patient learned as much as possible about how to think psychologically, and thus gained a sound base from which to work at understanding present and future fears, anxieties, and emotions?

Patients may raise the topic of termination *indirectly* in the form of a dream. Or, they may spend several sessions on reporting how well they feel and how well they are handling areas of difficulty. Patients may say they are thinking about moving out of town at some point in the future or are planning to change work schedules by taking on new responsibilities that will not allow as much time for therapy in the future, and so on. (These kinds of inferences can, of course, also be made by patients who are resisting treatment; however, for the purposes of this chapter, let us assume that your patient really does appear to be better and is getting ready to end.) The signal from the patient may also occur more *directly* by a question about how long therapy usually lasts or how termination will take place. Some patients may come right out and say that they are feeling better and have been thinking about ending their therapy.

Often patients do not know about the mechanics of ending and have been waiting for you to declare that they are "cured" or at least ready to begin thinking about stopping. When patients are being indirect, and sometimes even when they are being more direct, they may still deny that they have seriously been thinking about stopping when you first respond to the signal by saying: "I wonder if you've been having some thoughts about ending/cutting back your therapy?" This is because the thought of leaving the therapy relationship, even when one feels stronger and healthier, can sometimes be quite frightening.

ENDING

The beginning therapist, too, may get a little anxious when this topic is first introduced, not realizing that termination itself constitutes a whole other phase of therapy, and as such may go on for a considerable length of time. The fact that it has been mentioned means that it has come into the patient's mind as an idea and will continue to be a theme.

Termination thoughts and fantasies need to be explored with as much acceptance and care as the therapist gives to any other important issue in the patient's life. As has been mentioned, this is somewhat more difficult to accomplish, as the issue of ending necessarily involves the therapist in a personal sense. However, if you can continue to listen to your patient empathically, the topic of termination will ebb and flow just as other topics do in treatment, as the patient moves closer to working through and resolving it, gradually confirming that, in the light of everything they have talked about and are talking about, this is how they now wish to proceed. All the implications of ending the therapy relationship in terms of what you now know about your patient's history and current way of conducting their life need to be explored to the fullest, and many of your patient's subsequent behaviors, dreams, and feelings in the treatment now have to be seen, as it were, through your termination glasses.

No two terminations are alike, of course, and therefore it is difficult to describe exactly what will happen as you work through the beginning, middle, and end parts of the termination phase. Usually, as has been mentioned, patients will be working on current problems interwoven with the new issue of concluding their psychotherapy with you. In addition to this, one of the most predictable events that occurs during the termination phase, no matter how long it lasts, is that initial symptoms, chief complaints, and problem areas that may seem to have been resolved, or at least have received a lot of attention in the therapy, will reappear with a vengeance. It is almost as if the patient

ENDING

wants to challenge the idea that he or she really is better. This can be particularly disheartening for the therapist if it is not anticipated. Once you know that it may happen, you are then freer to explore with your patient the underlying meaning for the reemergence of the symptoms, rather than taking what the patient is saying at face value. Sometimes, as well, the reemergence of symptoms may be because your patient is ready to work on these problems at an even deeper level, finally resolving the last vestiges of the difficulties. At this point, he or she may be able to bring forward information about the problem never previously discussed. Another interesting occurrence during the ending phase is that a new issue may emerge. It never ceases to amaze me with my own patients, many of whom are women, how often an episode or even an ongoing course of sexual molestation is remembered close to the time of ending therapy. In response to my query, Why now?, the answer seems to be that it was the sense of this being the patient's "last chance" which had enabled the material to emerge from unconsciousness, or that the establishing of an ending time somehow mobilized the patient to become aware that there was more work to be done. Once it is out, patients generally seem surprised that an event as traumatic as sexual molestation could have been so completely repressed that they had almost undergone a whole psychotherapy without remembering it. Then time must be spent in dealing thoroughly with the "new" material and in integrating it into the rest of the psychotherapy insights and understandings.

At some point after the beginning of the termination phase, the patient and therapist should probably decide together on an actual date for the ending, with the patient taking the lead. However, it must be borne in mind that the patient may not be aware that ending will trigger additional feelings and sometimes totally new material. Therefore it is wise to be as generous as possible when negotiating a termination date to allow for the working through of the feelings and associations connected to it. If brand new material emerges after a termination date has already been set, then the possibility of prolonging the termination period has to be considered. Even if the "new" material is understood as a panic reaction to the idea of terminating, this is an indication that your patient is not feeling quite ready to end and may, legitimately, need more time. If the new material is something that he or she has not been able to remember (i.e., has not been conscious of) until the time for ending has been negotiated, then, as has been mentioned, the therapist must be flexible enough to disembark from the termination track for a while in order to help the patient understand and deal with this new information. It may be your impression, however, that your patient will never feel ready to end and needs some "encouragement." (I am reminded here of a cartoon in a recent *New Yorker* magazine where a psychoanalyst is pictured pushing a button which causes the couch to tilt forward so that the patient slides off.) Then, the reasons for the resistance to ending need to be explored and interpreted.

How to effect the ending can also be open to negotiation. Patients may be given the leeway to decide if they prefer a gradual cutting back, say from once weekly sessions to every second or third week for a while, or if they prefer to continue full throttle until the termination date. My preference is for the latter so that the feelings evoked by the termination are not diluted by the slowing down of the therapy. However, there is certainly something to say for the patient being able to end more comfortably, providing their feelings about leaving are not being avoided. Any cutting back, then, should only be done after the greater part of the patient's intense reactions to ending have been discussed. As well, some patients like to be given an appointment six months after termination. This may serve the

ENDING

following functions: (1) the patient is able to report to you "everything" that has taken place since leaving therapy; (2) the patient is satisfied that you are still there, and alive, in your office even though they are no longer with you; (3) they refresh their calming image of you; (4) they test out that they can contact you again, that the door has not been permanently closed; and (5) you appease your guilt about letting them go off into the outside world. Depending on your own life circumstances and your feelings about being recontacted, this is an option. However, despite all of the above, when the six-month checkup is actually carried out in practice, it is often experienced by both therapist and patient as quite anticlimactic.

The last session can be a difficult one for both the patient and the therapist; it is the therapist who should take the lead in terms of procedure. I usually start by stating gently that this is our last session, in case my patient has unconsciously planned to deny it until the very last moment, thereby not allowing enough time to say good-bye. Then, of course, I ask: "What feelings have you been having about today?" As these feelings are being talked about, it is interesting to note how your patient has been dealing with the actual time of ending. Some patients will have a flight into complete health, reassuring you and themselves that they are really fine now, that all their problems are more or less taken care of, and that they feel ready to tackle life. Part of the motivation for this may be a defense against the sadness or fear they may be feeling or it may constitute a wish to remain a "good patient" to the end. Some patients may feel overly scared or anxious at the thought of facing their life "alone," even though they have, in fact, been doing this for quite some time before ending. These patients may need to be reassured that there is life after termination! Probably the worst error you as a therapist can make at this point is to encourage the patient's dependency, thereby giving them the message that you, too, are not sure that

ENDING

they can handle what awaits them without you. Although you must listen empathically to their anxieties, it is also important now to give them the indication that you have confidence in them and that your expectation is that they will do just fine. Leaving the door open for further contact, should they require it at a future date and should you be able to provide it, can be done by simply stating: "You know where I am in case you need to talk to me again." I usually end the session with a warm handshake and a genuine wish that they will do well in life. Some patients will get teary when saying good-bye; this is to be expected. It is not expected that the therapist show any emotion other than warmth and well-wishing.

I would like to tell you about the termination of my patient, Ms. A, described briefly in chapter 1, the 35-year-old woman whose father had Alzheimer's disease. By profession a computer programmer, she had described herself at the beginning of her two years of treatment as not feeling connected to the world of people, but as being more at home in the world of nature. She felt that with people she always said the wrong things and spoke or laughed too loud so as to put others off. She was the type of individual who was never included in groups in high school, and even at university she had felt very unlikeable. To summarize a lot of important psychotherapy, as she was able to form a relationship with me, Ms. A began to nourish and value those parts of herself that were frank, honest, and highly energetic. She saw herself as someone with different ideas and, as such, someone who had a great deal to contribute at work. She became more relaxed and less intense socially and started to analyze her relationships with men vis-à-vis her relationship to her critical, demanding, but loving and exciting father. She saw how she chose men who were like him in some of the more negative ways that made her feel inadequate once in a relationship. It was with extreme pleasure that I watched the growth of this individual from "an unlikeable girl whom people avoided" to a self-confident woman who managed new and challenging situations with enthusiasm and humor. As an underlying theme throughout the treatment, Ms. A's father's health deteriorated. Never having allowed herself to cry much before, she began to be able to freely express the real pain and sadness she felt as she watched him slowly move toward this inhumane death. She acknowledged the bond that she had had with him, which was different from that of all the other family members; she acknowledged her intense anger at him and her deep love for him. In addition, she was also able, using appropriately what she had learned in her therapy, to be more helpful to her mother, as she became a nonjudgmental listener for her and her major source of support. Ms. A's request to cut back on her therapy sessions came while her father was still ill, after she had changed jobs to one requiring more responsibility and had been away on a holiday. She knew she felt much better, particularly in terms of her relationships with others where she now expected to be liked, instead of disliked.

We began to talk about the idea of ending treatment, and after some time, I agreed that meeting every two weeks would be appropriate, since we were both concerned about the imminent death of her father, which constituted an "extenuating" circumstance to her termination. About two months later, Ms. A met a man who, for the first time, made her feel good about herself and whom she felt she could be totally accepted by. She talked about this relationship during her bimonthly termination phase and made comments about the particular issues we had discussed, noticing when she was tending to fall back into old patterns she did not like. We had talked about her need to be able to let go of her father in order to really love another man, and she saw the fact that she had been able to meet the new man, even before her father actually died, as a sign that she had done the required work in her psychotherapy. Her father's death,

ENDING

when it came, while painful, did not tear her apart as she had expected. Shortly thereafter she announced that she was ready to leave treatment, and I agreed. We then set a date for ending. Although I felt sad saying good-bye to Ms. A, I felt good knowing that she was now able to handle the problems in her life in a different way.

The above discussion has been offered as a guide for how the termination of longer-term psychotherapy can be carried out. Often the endings do not go as smoothly as one would ideally wish, however, because they represent such a difficult time for both patient and therapist. Terminations can be stormy times, even if the patient is ready to leave treatment, or they can be impeded in some other way by the unresolved conflicts of the patient or the therapist. Sometimes, because feelings about ending have not been able to be completely worked through, either the patient or the therapist may be left feeling bereft or unsatisfied. At other times, there are external circumstances more or less out of our control that may interfere with our carrying out the completion of treatment in the manner we would wish.

It frequently happens for interns, for example, that *patients have to be terminated prematurely*, at least by a particular therapist, because a student's placement time in the setting is at an end. This never feels right for the patient, the student, or the supervisor, but at times it is unavoidable. In these situations the student will have already informed the patient of their internship or residency status at the very beginning of treatment and given the patient an idea of how long they will be able to see him or her in treatment. However, the information about how long the therapy can go on is often "forgotten" by the patient, and so when the time to end draws near, it may seem to come as a difficult and painful surprise. Patients, in this case, need to be reminded of the approaching termination date by their therapists, in order to have a reasonable amount of time for the

ENDING

working through of at least some of their feelings about ending treatment. Reasonableness depends on the length of time the therapy has lasted overall, with special sensitivity being given to patients who may have a history of abandonment by significant individuals in their lives.

For internship placements of nine months to one year, patients should be reminded about termination at least three months in advance. Student therapists may feel guilty about having to leave their patients in this way, that is because an internship is ending, and fearing their patient's rage, the student therapist will often collude consciously or unconsciously with the patient in not discussing their feelings about termination. It may be helpful to bear in mind that most people—therapists and patients alike—have some difficulty saying good-bye. For the patient, the ending will call up painful feelings about other endings or other losses in their life. Not dealing with your patient's feelings about stopping treatment with you is a disservice to the patient and cheats them out of a vital part of the psychotherapy. As has been stated previously, it is therefore extremely important to be continually wondering how your patient is reacting to the upcoming ending, what thoughts and fantasies the person may have about it, and what their plans are for the period immediately after termination. In fact, once it has been reintroduced, the eventuality of termination should be raised at *every* opportunity and should constitute a part of all of the therapist's conceptualizing and formulating of the patient's material and behavior henceforth (e.g., "I wonder if you're coming late/early to sessions because we talked about ending?"; "I wonder if you're avoiding that topic/raising this new topic because we have started to talk about ending treatment?").

Interestingly, some of the same phenomena that occur in more prolonged terminations, described earlier, will often occur in a more condensed manner in termination phases that are of shorter duration; for example, the intensifying of symptomatology or the opening up of new material. It is somewhat more difficult to manage these factors when there is a set time to end, and so they must be handled with even greater sensitivity. If symptoms do worsen in this type of situation, the therapist should attempt to determine what this reaction indicates. Is it a response to the early ending, with the symptom functioning as a more "acceptable" replacement for the patient's anger at having to terminate, or a symptom of the patient's fear or anxiety about leaving? Alternatively, there may be some other unconscious or perhaps transferential prototype for this occurrence. Once the patient's underlying motivations are exposed to the light and understood, this will always be the guide as to what steps can be taken to help the patient, for example, encouraging the patient to express anger more directly to you, if this is part of the problem.

If significant new material arises, then, of course, the possibility of your patient's continuing treatment with another therapist must be seriously considered. You may feel, in any case, that your patient will need more treatment after you leave; if this is so, then decisions need to be made with your supervisor far in advance of the termination date about whether another therapist can and should be offered to your patient at the time of ending treatment with you. If it is decided that another therapist is available to take on your patient, the specific details of this information should *not* be communicated to the patient until about two to three weeks before the actual termination day. Otherwise it may act as a tempting distraction for both the patient and the therapist from the patient's intense feelings about ending or may seem to the patient that they are being handed off to someone else without regard for their feelings. It is most therapeutic, therefore, to first offer your patient the opportunity to work through their feelings about ending with you, piece by piece, and then the possibility of referral to another therapist can be discussed.

If a patient leaves prematurely, either by telephoning to say they are stopping treatment, or simply not showing up for appointments, this can be particularly disastrous for the student therapist's self-esteem, especially if it has been entirely unpredicted. Beginning and intermediate therapists often take this as an indication that they are not competent, thinking that a more experienced therapist could have held onto the patient. It is important for the student therapist to keep in mind that *rarely* does a patient leave because of one empathic failure on the part of the therapist. If a working alliance has been established with the patient, there is usually room and flexibility in the relationship for the therapist to make a few errors, provided they are well-intentioned errors. A failure to understand the feelings of the patient about one certain incident, or a failure to have heard a particular story from the patient's perspective, may be a reason for temporary withdrawal, flight, or even anger on the part of the patient, but rarely termination. There are some patients, however, who are unable to express their anger in any other way than by leaving treatment. Sometimes this may be in response to the therapist's having left the patient for a vacation or other break, or in anticipation of a separation from the therapist or even termination (e.g., I'll leave you before you leave me). Sometimes the anger occurs in the context of a transference reaction and the therapist is being acted out against in the manner that individuals from the patient's past were dealt with or whom the patient wishes they had been able to act out against. Other types of patients may leave abruptly when the therapist is "getting to them" in some way, for example, when they feel intense erotic or dependent feelings for the therapist which frighten them, or when the therapist has managed to get beyond psychological defenses that have never been threatened before. In this case, the patient may regret having told the therapist "too much" or being "too vulnerable" and may be protecting themselves by leaving therapy.

If your patient has not shown up for more than one session without explanation or if he or she leaves a telephone message canceling future sessions, then you should telephone the patient to encourage him or her to return for at least one more session to discuss their reasons for leaving. This "last" session can be an extremely productive one as the exploration that is conducted in it helps the therapist to understand what caused the patient to react as they did, and also helps the patient to understand their own underlying motivations. In addition, once some light has been shed on your patient's reasons for ending and once they have the experience of seeing that they could want to stop treatment and will still not be rejected by you, and that their anger, or panic, or even dissatisfaction with the treatment can be tolerated and understood, then they may want a second chance to continue their therapy. If the patient will not come in to talk about ending, then a *brief* discussion on the telephone might be helpful in shedding some light on why the termination occurred in the manner it did. In supervision, your temptation might be to gloss over this premature ending quickly and move on to the next patient. However, it is imperative for your feelings about yourself as a therapist with the next patient and all future patients that time be spent now on trying to analyze and understand the reasons for this patient's departure.

Termination is a challenging time for all therapists. As a student therapist, because of the availability of supervision, it can be an excellent learning opportunity which should be taken full advantage of. As Basch (1980) has said:

> There is no way one can ever do a "complete" job in either psychotherapy or psychoanalysis. It is impossible to anticipate everything the patient may encounter in the future and to prepare him for it.

ENDING

All that therapy can do is to help the patient understand himself sufficiently so that when he is faced with the inevitable stresses of life, he does not simply repeat old defensive patterns but, instead, exercises choice in his response based on the present and past significance of the situation at hand [p. 52].

After the therapy has ended, it is important to write a *termination note* which will be put on the patient's chart. The termination note should include the following: (1) the patient's chief complaint(s) when he or she first came for treatment; (2) your formulation of the problem(s) and of your patient's psychodynamics at that time; (3) a summary of the treatment themes and the progress of treatment (one to two paragraphs); (4) the reasons for termination, and your agreement or lack of agreement; (5) further disposition, if any. The note should be written so that a new psychotherapist could continue with this patient, if necessary, and understand briefly what transpired in the patient's previous therapy.

It is interesting, and perhaps somewhat reassuring to the therapist, to be aware that there is often a *posttermination* phase experienced by most patients who have been in psychoanalytically oriented psychotherapy. During the first few months after ending, some patients may still have feelings of sadness and loss, and the occasional time where it is only you that they want to describe certain events to. As well, however, there appears to be *more* healing that takes place after therapy has ended. Often patients will proceed farther with their growth, sometimes resolving issues they were unable to resolve completely in their treatment or even clearing up symptoms that were not entirely taken care of. They usually are able to take on even more responsibility and get even more pleasure out of their lives several months after termination than they were at the actual time of stopping their treatment. This may be partly due to the residual effects of the treatment, and to their being able to hold inside

ENDING

of them the therapeutic relationship with you, and partly due to the positive message that comes from being able to end treatment: the sense of being better, of being independent, and of no longer requiring psychotherapy.

FLAGGING THE TRANSFERENCE DURING TERMINATION

The termination phase is often a fertile time for the mobilization of transference responses, some of them old transferences revisited and some of them new ones. As has been mentioned earlier, feelings of loss and abandonment that you may have noticed at other times of separation from your patient, during vacations or even the endings of each session, will undoubtedly be prominent at this time of concluding therapy. Even though it may have been your patient who has raised the topic of ending, he or she may be feeling abandoned by you. Therefore knowing your patient's history in terms of losses and separation is of extreme importance in predicting transference responses at this time. One example of a transference reaction during termination was mentioned in the section on free association in chapter 5 (p. 78), where a patient of mine, who was ending therapy, had the tune *She's Leaving Home* on her mind. Exploration of this gave information about her specific transference experience during termination. Because you are in the "real" situation of stopping a relationship, the transferential responses will at times be related to this, and at times be displacements from figures from the past. Therefore, as was mentioned earlier in this chapter, once the idea of ending has come up, all further material must be assessed in the light of it, and in the light of the patient's transferential responses to it.

As another example, when my patient, Mr. G, the 39-year-old businessman introduced in chapter 5 who had problems with commitment in relationships, raised the idea of terminating his therapy, he was obviously feeling well and wanted to try out his gains, particularly in the area of sexuality, which we had been discussing in detail—without having to report them in his treatment. As we talked about when exactly he might want to end, he began for the first time to become quite flirtatious with me. I pointed this out and asked him specifically what his relating to me in this way had to do with *ending treatment*. He was able to think about it for a while and then said he supposed that he had been reverting back to his earlier behavior where he "used to flirt a lot with a woman before dumping her"! This led to a rich discussion which helped reinforce his insights about his sexuality and himself in relationships. If this behavior had occurred at a different time in the therapy, obviously we both might have thought about a different interpretation.

When a symptom worsens during termination, or when new material emerges, alongside of these issues having to be worked with in the treatment as described earlier, possible manifestations of transference reactions have to be considered. For example, the worsening of a symptom may indicate hostility toward the therapist or a clinging dependency, not yet fully analyzed in treatment. The meaning of the symptom and its relation to important others in the patient's life has to be reexplored so that its significance in the patient's not getting well, or as a cry for more help, can be understood. Of course patients can act out in a variety of ways during termination, including coming late, missing sessions, bringing in friends, or sometimes pets, to meet you (I have met two cats and one dog during this time!), being unable to leave at the end of sessions, engaging in flights during therapy time, and so on. All of these resistances to dealing with feelings about ending and possible transferences will have to be commented on and interpreted in the context of this ending and of past endings in the patient's life.

Sometimes patients will refer another patient to you, usually a close friend, either before or just after termination. If it is before the ending occurs, then the opportunity to understand

and interpret the behavior exists and the referral should not be accepted until this has been done, and possibly not at all. The most common reason for this type of referral usually is to provide you with a substitute for your ending patient. This is because your patient feels that he or she will be missed so much that you will need to fill their spot immediately or because this new patient may serve as a reminder of the terminating patient for you, and the terminating patient will be able to continue his or her treatment by proxy. It could also be that the suggested referral is a test of whether you are wishing for another, "younger sibling" of the patient to replace and displace them, or even of whether you have not got enough patients to see and need this patient to help you fill your practice! Your patient may imagine that the referral gives him or her power over you and over the new patient–friend. It is also sometimes interesting to see what type of patient your terminating patient decides to refer—is the person similar to or different from the patient?

There are patients who, in striving to hold onto the therapy by identifying with you, will decide at or near termination that they have become interested in your profession, for example, psychology. They may actually begin taking psychology courses before the ending date comes or may in other ways begin the process of planning a career change to this area. Besides possibly expressing a need to identify with you, this may be an indication of their envy of you, of feelings of sibling rivalry with you, or of a combination of all three. In this situation it may be particularly difficult to interpret the underlying motivations to the patient because they may experience the interpretation as discouragement from pursuing this work. They may believe you think they are not bright enough to study in this field, that you do not want them as a colleague, or that you see them as having too many emotional problems to become, for example, a psychologist. There may be times, as well, when your patient has learned so

ENDING

much from the treatment and has enjoyed thinking psychologically to such an extent that they legitimately want to see if they are suited for a profession in this or a related area. In either case, the feelings, wishes, and fantasies about studying psychology or a similar field have to be explored, and the question of their relationship to your work has to be posed. Usually, once patients have had time to explore the thought thoroughly, they will arrive at what seems to be the best decision.

Another transference reaction that sometimes emerges during the termination phase and is particularly difficult for students to handle is the patient's suggestion that the relationship be carried on in a different form after termination. For example, a patient may say: "Since we're both students at the same university, why couldn't we meet for coffee once in a while?" Or, "I'd like to bring you a copy of that book I've been reading—how about if I drop it by sometime?" The answer to all such overtures must be no. Of course you would not give this answer immediately without exploring the motivation for the request and after doing this, no answer may be needed as the patient understands the reasons for the behavior and no longer needs to act them out. If the motivation for the overture is to prolong the therapy relationship under the guise of "friendship," then what the patient may want is more caretaking by you and more one-sided conversation with you as the empathic listener.

The motivation for a "friendship" could also be so that the patient can "prove" that he or she was, indeed, your favorite patient. This may relate to feelings of sibling rivalry. It is usually best to explain at these times that what has gone on here has not been a friendship because its purpose has been to focus only on the patient, with your knowledge and expertise applied to this task. Turning the relationship into a friendship would be disappointing to your patient because they would no longer be entitled to this kind of focus. If it is appropriate, you can reiterate that you do not become friends with your patients because you want to remain there for them as a potential therapist, should they ever need to see you again. They can go out into the world and make many friends, especially with the insight of what they now seem to know they need in a friendship, that is, an accepting and nonjudgmental individual, and you will still be here as their therapist. If the purpose for prolonging the relationship is curiosity about you, something that may emerge more strongly as termination of treatment is discussed, then the transference fantasies can be explored with questions such as: "What do you imagine I am like at university?" "What is your fantasy about the friendships I have?" and so on. The displacements from individuals from the patient's past and the projections of what the patient wishes for him- or herself will in this way be brought to light. Sometimes the ending patient's need to establish a special after-therapy relationship with you may involve unresolved oedipal wishes which are being acted out: "I've got mommy/daddy all to myself now." These types of responses from patients usually indicate a resistance to ending treatment, another avenue you and your patient must explore.

It is extremely important to discuss the issue of "friendship" with the patient in your supervision. Some students feel obliged to honor their patients' requests so as not to reject them. Some feel flattered that the patient wants to meet them afterwards. Interns also may feel it is the only "democratic" thing to do, and the thought gives them a tremendous feeling of relief that they can finally stop being such a powerful person in the patient's life and relate to them more on a par. All of these countertransference thoughts and feelings, and more, can be examined with your supervisor.

Transference reactions, then, must be flagged and decisions made until the very end of the therapy about whether to uncover their history and interpret them. They will continue to provide

ENDING

fascinating material for the understanding of your patient's dynamics, so long as you can allow yourself to be utilized as a transference object and can work hand-in-hand with your patient at exploring and understanding them together in an accepting manner.

7.

Special Challenges Patients Present

Although there are always challenging patients for every level of psychotherapist, there are particular challenges that beginning therapists face with certain patients that can be quite tricky to manage. In actuality, these are not "personality types" and certainly not DSM diagnoses; rather, they are types of *defenses* that patients employ, particularly when they are in anxiety-provoking situations like psychotherapy, that seem to characterize them. Some of these are listed below; undoubtedly the readers of this book, after a little experience, will be able to add to this list.

THE "BRIGHT" PATIENT

This patient has fortified him- or herself before coming for therapy by reading several books on psychological theory (sometimes more than you have read) and begins early in treatment, often in the first session, by asking you in a rather challenging manner to describe your theoretical orientation. Students often falter here because, if the truth be known, they have not, and should not yet have, a firm theoretical orientation; this is why they are students, to learn about various ways of doing psychotherapy. Although the question can certainly be examined in

SPECIAL CHALLENGES PATIENTS PRESENT

more depth later on, this is probably not the time to say: "I wonder why you're asking me this now?" This may indeed be the way your patient defends against the fear of having to be "weak" or "emotional," if that is what they imagine being in psychotherapy will be like. However, as a consumer, the patient legitimately deserves a direct answer this time. In response to this, some students will try to describe the orientation of their current supervisor, which is not entirely a mistake since the ensuing therapy will be conducted more or less from that point of view. Using the word *eclectic* was enough to satisfy patients in the early eighties, but does not hold as much water today. If you are conducting psychodynamically oriented psychotherapy, as is being discussed in this book, the best way to describe it is probably as a historical form of treatment. You can explain that you will be asking questions about the patient's history and family background and that it is from this perspective that you will be trying to gain an understanding of their personality structure or dynamics and their current difficulties. You might also say that there will be sessions when the two of you will focus on the present, but also times when the two of you will talk about the patient's past, and how what happened then has affected their life. You may also want to add that you are not a directive therapist and will be listening to what they want to tell you so that together you can understand the problems and, you hope, help to make some changes. After all of this has been said, probably the longest "speech" you will ever make in therapy, it is imperative to get your patient's reaction to what you have said. Some patients may not have understood much of the information, despite having appeared to be so knowledgeable at first. Some may react negatively, or may want to ask more questions. For some patients, just hearing you talk will have given them time to adjust to the therapy situation and may have had a calming effect, irrespective of what you have actually said.

SPECIAL CHALLENGES PATIENTS PRESENT

THE "DUMB" PATIENT

This patient seems not to know anything about how psychotherapy is conducted and about what might be expected of them. Even though this type of patient may be well educated, he or she behaves as though you are a genius and every word you say is far more brilliant than anything they could ever have thought of. There is the feeling of strained idealization because it does not ring true. This may be a defense against your patient's own need to control the session or against a fear that a student therapist may not be able to help them (in both of these cases, the defense employed would be reaction formation), or it may be a defense simply against the anxiety of the therapy situation. In any case, it is best to gently point out to the patient that they appear to be feeling a little anxious and perhaps would like to talk about that. It is important that you try to understand the motivation for this particular type of defense, and how the patient's self-depreciating behavior is undoubtedly played out in other parts of their life as well.

THE CONDESCENDING PATIENT

Early in treatment, this patient frequently alludes, either directly or indirectly, to your student status, and with some condescension. He or she may ask who your supervisor is and what their orientation is, and then may make comments like: "I guess you'll have to discuss this one with your supervisor," when describing a difficult problem. Or, "What did your supervisor think about what we talked about last week?" Most probably this is not your patient's first awareness that they are being seen by a student therapist. In most clinics, patients are informed of this and agree to it in advance of their first session. In some cases, these patients may actually be having trouble with the fact that a supervisor, or authority type individual, lurks in the background, and their

SPECIAL CHALLENGES PATIENTS PRESENT

transference may at first be manifesting itself more to this "parental" figure. Sometimes the patient may be having difficulty with the idea of seeing a student because they may feel that deep down they are really "sick" and may need a lot of help. In these situations, because the defense seems particularly annoying to the student therapist, it is best to confront it head on by saying: "Have you noticed that you refer to my supervisor quite a lot? Tell me what thoughts you are having about him or her." Or, "I wonder if my being a student has given you some concern. Why don't you tell me more about that." Always remember that these behaviors are defenses; as such they are protecting the patient against some undesirable feeling like anxiety. They are not to be taken at face value as if the patient really would prefer to be treated by your supervisor, but to be understood together in the context of the patient's life.

THE INTRUSIVE PATIENT

This patient tries to discover as much about you as a person as possible. He or she may start with the most obvious, "I see by the fact that you wear a wedding ring that you are married . . ." and move on from there. Nothing escapes this patient's notice—your hairdo, your clothing, the pictures in your office—and they will often ask direct questions that make you feel uncomfortable. I once had a patient, for example, who, after going to a great deal of difficulty to determine what kind of car I drove (i.e., by examining my car keys which happened to be on my desk) and watching to see where I parked, then commented in almost every session about my car (e.g., "You parked very close to the exit today; or, "I notice you had such-and-such a theater program inside your car—did you see that play?").

Sometimes the intrusiveness may come across as critical, as your patient seems so intent on "sizing you up." It rarely is done for purposes of criticism. This is a style some patients learn in their families of origin as a way of being "close." For others it may be a way of controlling the session or of trying to identify with you in a rather desperate way. One of the so-called postures required of psychoanalytically oriented psychotherapists is that of anonymity, and the intrusive patient makes this particularly difficult for some students to achieve. As Greenson (1967) put it: "There is no doubt that the less the patient really knows about the psychoanalyst, the more easily he can fill in the blank spaces with his own fantasies" (p. 274). Students often feel that they are depriving a patient or being cold or impersonal by not answering their patient's questions about themselves and their personal lives. When they try to follow their supervisor's advice to put the question back into the patient's court, by asking about the motivation and timing of the question, many students feel they are withholding or putting themselves "above" the patient. However, the most therapeutic way to deal with this type of defense is to observe: "I notice that you are quite concerned about what I wear/my hair, etc. Why don't we talk a little more about that." Or, "You seem quite observant about others. Tell me how you are feeling about being in therapy with me."

THE ENTERTAINING PATIENT

This patient is initially experienced as a delight, someone who brightens your day and whom you look forward to seeing; that is, of course, until you have met with your supervisor. This patient is witty and actually tells jokes that are funny, obviously needing the response of laughter from you. He or she may have learned that they have talent for this and that it helps to make them feel more comfortable in anxiety-laden situations as well as making it easy for people to like them. I once treated a couple in marital therapy who could have been a comedy team. Together they played off each other in the beginning of each session to entertain me, as they must have done often in social situations with very positive results. However, one of the partners had had an extramarital affair and they were in treatment to see if the marriage could survive it. When I (reluctantly) made the observation that they used this behavior as a resistance against talking about their very painful marital difficulties, they were able to catch themselves when they started it and for the most part to stop spending their valuable therapy time in this way. As we talked more about it, it emerged that each of the partners individually used humor at difficult times in their lives and that, in fact, the other's sense of humor was a large part of the initial attraction to each other. This revelation seemed to nourish their attempts at feeling good about each other again.

THE SEDUCTIVE PATIENT

This patient usually operates most effectively in an opposite-sex patient–therapist combination; however, same-sex combinations can also be fertile ground for the manifestation of this defense. In this situation, the patient is being deliberately provocative trying to get a sexually aroused response from the therapist. They may dress in a provocative way and/or may sit in a provocative posture during the session, watching to see if you are looking. They may also bring in dreams laden with sexual content or describe sexual material in a highly erotic manner. For example, one of my female students recently treated a female patient who seemed to be continually describing ongoing sexual molestation in an erotic way, which was very difficult for her therapist to listen to. After the first several times the material had been gone over in depth, we began to notice that this material was raised at certain points in the therapy, when the patient was feeling bad about herself and when she craved more involvement from her therapist. Being "sexual" was the way she had elicited a response from others in her past and she was repeating it in her therapy. Students may be particularly vulnerable to this

SPECIAL CHALLENGES PATIENTS PRESENT

kind of behavior simply because of lack of experience in dealing with it. Discussing your countertransferential responses in supervision can also be difficult; however, doing so will help you to remain neutral in the therapy situation so as not to fall into the response patterns that have historically been instrumental in producing this problem for your patient.

THE PATIENT WHO WILL NOT LEAVE

Ending sessions can sometimes be difficult for beginning therapists, as has been mentioned in chapters 2 and 5. There are certain types of patients who make it particularly hard for therapists to end by looking wistfully at them when the fact that time is up is announced, by starting a new and interesting or very emotional topic in the last five minutes of the session, or simply by not getting up out of their chair when the ending has come. These patients may perceive the ending of each session as a rejection. As the therapist, you may then feel guilty about ending a session, especially when your patient has just burst into a flood of tears, and you may want to give "more" to your patient by going overtime. If the emotions that your patient is expressing are genuine and unusual, then, of course you may have to go a few minutes overtime once or twice. However, if your patient makes a habit of starting emotional topics near the end of the session or on the way out the door, or if they are reluctant to get up even though you may already be standing, then this behavior is certainly worth analyzing. As was mentioned earlier, you must take control and end the session in a firm but gentle manner: "Our time is up for today. I know what you're saying right now is very important, so let's give it more time next week." Then, at the *beginning* of the next session, the therapist can comment: "Have you noticed that you seem to start talking about important topics just as we are ready to end? Let's talk about that." Or, "Have you noticed that you sometimes feel reluctant

SPECIAL CHALLENGES PATIENTS PRESENT

to leave here? Tell me what you're feeling as the end of our time together approaches." Starting with the words "have you noticed" introduces the element of partnership to the patient who becomes an observer, too, so that they will not feel criticized. This begins an exploration which may be a theme for the next several sessions. Sometimes these patients will spontaneously reveal, for example, that they have trouble ending telephone conversations as well, or leaving friends' homes after a visit, or that in the past, they felt they never had enough time with important people in their lives. This, of course, tips you off to valuable transference data, such as how you are being experienced as the session draws to a close. Bringing this material to light will help your patient to understand and probably start to change behaviors they may not like in themselves.

THE PATIENT WHO WANTS TO LEAVE TOO SOON

These patients also anticipate the ending of a session as a rejection, but have the attitude of: "I'll get out of here before you have a chance to reject me." They may sit on the edge of their chair for the last five minutes of the session ready to bolt out the door as soon as the time is up. One of the interns I supervised was treating a woman for whom rejection was a life-long theme. This patient had spent so much of her early years trying to avoid being rejected by her mother and sisters that her avoidance behavior seemed like an unconscious "reflex" reaction. Approximately seven minutes before the end of each session, she would put on her jacket and sunglasses while she continued to talk to her therapist! A highly educated and competent woman, she herself did not notice anything unusual in her behavior until it was pointed out to her. Other patients who fall into this category may be trying to take the control of the session away from the therapist by being the one to declare that the session has come to an end. Another intern I supervised was treating a patient

SPECIAL CHALLENGES PATIENTS PRESENT

who did this in a rather condescending manner. She would look at her watch, sometimes yawn, and then say: "Well, I have to go now . . ." implying she had a very busy schedule, and left her therapist still grappling with whatever material she had most recently brought up. Although the therapist's countertransference response was somewhat different in this case than with the patient first described, the underlying motivation for each patient of avoiding the rejection still played the major part with the added defense of needing to take control in a situation where both patients must have felt quite out of control.

THE "SCARY" PATIENT

This patient talks about aggression and aggressive fantasies and sometimes behaves aggressively in the session by raising their voice either directly in relation to the therapist or indirectly under the guise of describing anger felt toward someone else. Student therapists have most difficulty with this when the patient is male and the therapist female. This type of patient often evokes a countertransferential response in the supervisor as well who usually feels protective of the student therapist. Discussion of your responses to your patient in supervision is particularly important here, as these patients can intimidate therapists into not giving interpretations due to fear of aggressive retaliation; unfortunately then the aggressive behavior may be reinforced. It may be difficult to remember with these patients that the aggression is a defense and that your patient may be feeling quite frightened. The following interventions could be tried: "Have you noticed you are raising your voice to me? Can you tell me how you are feeling right now?" Or, "I'm wondering why you are spending so much of your time in here talking about how you would like to hurt people. Is this something you think about a lot when you are alone?" This latter will give you information as to whether the aggression is a transferential reaction

SPECIAL CHALLENGES PATIENTS PRESENT

or an ongoing current problem for your patient. If you continue to feel frightened with your patient, then it may indeed be that this patient cannot benefit from a psychodynamic therapy. A referral to another therapist and possibly another type of treatment should be considered.

THE OVERLY GRATEFUL/UNGRATEFUL PATIENT

The overly grateful patient seems particularly satisfying initially, especially to the student therapist who wants to "help" people. This patient makes statements like: "I couldn't have gotten through that family visit without our talk of last week." Or, "I'm so glad to be here, I was counting the days." Or, "I thought about everything you said to me and you were so right—I never would have thought of it that way by myself." Unfortunately, this is sometimes a reaction formation and what your patient really is feeling is the opposite, that you are not helping him or her enough. This type of attitude could also be masking a beginning dependency that this patient hopes you will never escape from. For some patients, this is a way of getting others to like them, by making them feel important and needed. It is imperative, of course, to first discover the underlying motivation for the behavior, and then to identify it as a relational style, and together with your patient, explore its antecedents.

The ungrateful patient will never give credit to you or to the therapy, even though it is perfectly clear that it is mainly because of their treatment that they have been able to make certain advances. These patients may say: "I don't know why I'm feeling better lately." Or, "Thank goodness I have so-and-so in my life, I don't know what I'd do without them. I can tell them everything." It is as if your presence—not to mention all your hard work—has gone completely unnoticed. Even when you ask directly: "What do you think has helped you to be able to deal with your mother?" These patients may say, "I don't know. I

SPECIAL CHALLENGES PATIENTS PRESENT

guess she's changing somehow." This can be extremely frustrating for the student therapist who, at least now and then, may need some evidence that therapy is having some effect. For these patients, however, acknowledging that their treatment is working, or even that they have a relationship with you, may be too threatening. It is as if they will have given something away, and they would then feel exquisitely vulnerable to rejection or hurt by you. The patient described earlier (p. 128) who put on her sunglasses before the end of every session, also announced to her therapist, after several months of treatment, that there was "no relationship" here. As the therapy moved along, she was able to liken it to going to the dentist, with the same type of relationship as she had there. It is usually best not to intervene directly in this behavior but rather to see your patient's ability to bring you into their world as a measuring stick of their being able to form a new, somewhat dependent relationship in which they have to trust another individual. As such patients start to feel better about themselves and about the idea of being in the therapy relationship with you, and less fearful of rejection, they will slowly be able to give indications that you and the psychotherapeutic work are, indeed, important.

THE CARETAKING PATIENT

This patient seems concerned about your state of health, fatigue, and so on, almost more than about their own. Sometimes this type of patient will bring you a coffee every session, or they may comment sympathetically that you are looking tired or hassled. These patients have such difficulty taking anything from others that they must always try to give something in return. It could also be that your patient may be feeling such low self-esteem that they feel the only way they could be tolerated would be to bring you a gift each time to make up for their presence. Tempting as it may be at times to allow your patient to look after you,

SPECIAL CHALLENGES PATIENTS PRESENT

for example, to tell them you've just been up all night studying for an exam, of course there is no way that this should happen. Instead, after thanking them for the coffee or their concern, you could observe that they seem to feel they need to look after others and ask if they are finding it difficult to allow themselves to be looked after in their therapy. Your task as the therapist is to focus only on your patients and their needs and the motivations for their behavior, as has been stated several times in this book. Your patients' psychotherapy is not the place to get your own needs met.

THE OLDER PATIENT

Along the same lines as the above, there are times when students are assigned patients who are considerably older than themselves who may trigger certain countertransference reactions that make doing psychotherapy more difficult. If the patient is close enough in age to a parent, then the student therapist may have a parental transferential response to his or her patient, sometimes unconsciously expecting to be looked after by the patient, sometimes feeling tentative about exploring emotional topics with the patient (i.e., not wanting to see them cry), or sometimes feeling angry at the patient for not handling their life better (after all, the patient is old enough to know how to deal with bosses, relationships, etc.). Sexual issues may be avoided because the student therapist may unconsciously not want to hear about the older patient's sexual life or problems. There are also times when student therapists may be overly kind or sweet to older patients in an effort to compensate for the fact that they have been unable to have warm and satisfying relationships with their own parents. All of the above are conscious and sometimes unconscious transference and countertransference responses of the therapist that should be worked through in supervision as much as possible. If they are not discussed in an ongoing way

SPECIAL CHALLENGES PATIENTS PRESENT

with your supervisor, you will find that your ability to conduct psychodynamic psychotherapy will be seriously impaired and both you and your patient will lose out.

THE PATIENT WHO SEEMS JUST LIKE YOU

It may happen that during the first few sessions with a new patient, the student therapist may have the feeling that this patient is exactly like them. This may relate to the patient's age, sex, upbringing, sense of humor, personality type, or sometimes to their actual presenting problems. The therapist then thinks: This patient has the same problems as me, if I can't solve my own, how am I ever going to be able to help this person? Again we are presented here with a countertransference reaction which your innocent patient will fall victim to if you do not identify it and deal with it in your supervision. It rarely happens that patients actually are that much like us, or like any other patient for that matter. The feeling of "sameness," which for some therapists may be a defense against their anxiety in conducting therapy or a method for beginning to empathize with the patient, soon eases up as you get to know your patient and his or her idiosyncrasies better. In other words, as your patient becomes a person to you, although you may still see similarities, you will also be quite aware of the differences between you. Still, if your patient presents with a similar problem to one you are currently struggling with, this does not necessarily mean that you cannot be helpful to him or her. The main pitfall here is in assuming your patient feels the exact same way about having the problem as you do or that the difficulty is manifested for them in the same way as it is for you. If you can put your version of the problem aside and really listen to your patient, it is certainly possible that you can be of great assistance to them. For example, I once supervised an intern who himself had an airplane phobia, but who managed to successfully treat a female patient with that

SPECIAL CHALLENGES PATIENTS PRESENT

presenting problem. Although I hesitate to write this as it can be abused and is *never* one of the goals of therapy, it is also possible that you will get some help with your problem from having worked with your patient on the same issue. (The intern I supervised above, however, still has his plane phobia.)

THE "PERFECT" PATIENT

Not to be confused with the immediately preceding category, this type of patient behaves in such a way as to cause absolutely no difficulties and to never incur any bad feeling of any sort. He or she always arrives on time and leaves easily. There are never additional demands made on the therapist, and, as if they had read this very book before coming, they never fall into any of the dreaded categories listed above. This patient listens to your comments and interpretations and seems to be giving them a great deal of thought both in the session and in the time between sessions. He or she shows appropriate affect when talking about emotional issues and never gives the therapist any hassles about holidays or other breaks. This patient readily agrees to having sessions taped, to being the subject of case conferences, and, in general, to going along with whatever you suggest. It is particularly difficult to identify this type of patient, other than that they seem so pleasant to be with, and therefore it may take considerably longer to identify this as a defensive style; however, as you describe them in supervision, it may come to light that they are being too perfect. Keeping in mind that the therapy is for the patient and not the therapist, we do not want patients to repeat old behaviors with us that they may not have even tried to evaluate. Many of these types of patients have come from families where one or both parents were extremely critical of them and they learned to protect themselves from that criticism by never doing anything to incur it. These patients may feel that their "real" self is nowhere near as perfect as the one they show you, and they are very certain that you would despise it, just as others in the past have done. Sometimes this type of patient has a "secret" that they think is particularly awful and that they are striving to cover up. Intervening with the patient who manifests this type of defense is often a delicate matter. I usually wait until the working alliance is more clearly established and the patient is starting to trust me. Then, naturally, there will occur times when the patient cannot be as perfect as they want to be, and the therapist then gets an opportunity to make a comment showing how accepting they would be of *any* part of their patient ("I notice you have never sworn before this. Were you feeling I couldn't accept the part of you who swears?") Thus, there may be a very small "lapse" which can change the whole climate of the therapy; sometimes patients, feeling more trusting of you, will consciously or unconsciously arrange for these lapses so that they can show more of their real selves and see what happens.

One of my patients, a male executive whose job was being threatened, always came to sessions dressed in a suit and tie and was very careful about how he worded his complaints. After about four months of this, he appeared one day in casual clothes with an old and torn, obviously well-loved, cap on his head. He apologized profusely for his attire, stating that he was going to a baseball game after our session. During the hour, he was far more relaxed than he had ever been and was able to elaborate on and become emotional about the negative parts of himself that were costing him his job. In the next session, he appeared in his regular attire and, unfortunately, had returned to his earlier defensive style. When I pointed this out and implied that I had found him more approachable during the session with the cap, he seemed genuinely grateful and then said he was afraid to be that way at work, but was willing to consider that maybe others might respond more positively to this side of him than he had previously thought. That session was always referred to by us subsequently as the "session with the cap," and helped as a reminder for him of the parts of his self that he had thought were unacceptable to others.

Are there any patients, you may be asking yourself, who do not manifest defenses that put them into a "category"? Fortunately for us, patients are always challenging us and our own humanness in many, many ways. This is part of what makes conducting psychotherapy such a fascinating and insightful experience for the therapist. No one would want a patient who does not manifest some type of defensive behavior, or is too perfect. In fact, patients who seem defenseless at first or who attach themselves too easily, may not have the ego strengths and boundaries to be able to benefit from psychodynamic psychotherapy. The above descriptions are included so that student therapists will be alerted to some of the many potential challenges and take advantage of their supervision time to learn how to understand and work with them.

8.

Using Supervision

Supervision has had a great deal of mention throughout this book because it is seen by this author as an extremely important and valuable learning opportunity which, if made use of correctly, can be of enormous benefit to the student therapist. Schwartz and Abel (1955) stated that "The heart of the education of the psychoanalytic psychotherapist, apart from personal analysis, is supervised clinical experience" (p. 257). A clear introduction to different methods of supervision and its structural aspects is offered in another early paper by Wagner (1957). In fact, there are several very early articles on dynamics in the supervision setting that might be of interest to the reader, including those by Knight (1945), Kelly (1951), and Hutt (1953).

Of course supervision, especially in the beginning with a new supervisor, can be extremely anxiety-provoking, and most supervisors are very aware of this. The student is put in the unique and certainly difficult position of being a part of two emotionally charged relationships at the same time, having to shift from being the helper to being the one who is asking for help, and where everything he or she says and does is being scrutinized by the individuals on both sides. In addition to this, unconscious forces are being mobilized in the therapist as well as in both the individuals to whom he or she is relating. How then, you ask, can anyone relax enough to learn in this situation?

USING SUPERVISION

Let us examine what goes on step-by-step. Often before meeting your supervisor, you may have heard through the student grapevine some "information" about him or her. This information usually revolves around the way that supervisor interacts with their interns, for example, tough, supportive, and so on. Sometimes interns get to choose their supervisors; at other times they are assigned. Because the supervisory situation is set up not only as a place to get help with your patient but also as a place from which you will be evaluated on your psychotherapy skills, it is quite natural to feel that you want to make a good impression on your supervisor and, unfortunately, to be somewhat defensive, at least initially. This, of course, will affect the way you present your patient to the supervisor. It may be helpful to realize that the supervisor–student relationship is just that, a *relationship*; as such it will be different for different students, and sometimes with different patients. Because of this, it is really difficult to predict how you will get along with your supervisor until you are actually in the relationship. It is also reassuring to know that most supervisor–student relationships run quite smoothly and that here the student therapist can feel nurtured, taught, and understood in the deepest sense of the word. These relationships often carry on long after the student has become a colleague, with the supervisor and the intern maintaining a somewhat special status in each other's professional lives.

Most supervisors of psychodynamically oriented psychotherapy structure supervisory sessions in a way that is somewhat analogous to the way the therapy is carried out; that is, they establish a set time to meet, usually once a week, with the meetings lasting approximately one hour. The student therapist is expected to be committed to that time, and to make it a priority, not canceling unless it is unavoidable. This provides you with a protected space in your supervisor's schedule, a time when he or she will be there to listen to you and to help you with your patient or patients.

USING SUPERVISION

The contract of the supervisory sessions is, essentially, that the student therapist will communicate to the supervisor what has transpired in the therapy hour. Mutual discussion will ensue, with guidelines, and sometimes interpretations, being offered by the supervisor which one hopes lead to a better understanding of the patient and of the therapeutic process. Different supervisors employ different methods of hearing the data from the psychotherapy session. As was mentioned at the beginning of this book, I like to have student therapists tape their sessions and then I listen carefully to the tapes, making extensive notes as I listen, the rationale being that I will not only hear the words but the feeling and tone of the session and also be able to begin to pick up countertransference difficulties if they exist. As Kubie (1958) has stated, tape recordings have the following advantages: they never make up anything; they allow for the study of the implications of words, changes in volume, interaction, and affective attitudes; and they are self-revelatory to the student, giving the opportunity to become aware of subtle nuances. Other supervisors, particularly supervisors of psychoanalytic students, prefer to have the student therapist verbally describe the details of the session, feeling that the way in which the session is reported, what is left out, what is emphasized, and so on provides significant data as to the flow of the therapy and also as to the student's countertransference. Some supervisors require extensive written notes which they ask to see before the supervisory session. Whatever way it is done, it is important that you try to communicate to your supervisor, with as much honesty as is consciously possible, what went on in the session between you and your patient.

Fleming (1953) has outlined three types of learning occurring in the supervision experience: imitative learning or learning by identification, where the student completely identifies with the supervisor's approach; "corrective learning" where, by discussing dynamics, the supervisor will be able to help the intern clarify their understanding of the patient so as to arrive at a more accurate interpretation of the patient's behavior; and "creative learning" where students are taught to ask questions of themselves (e.g., "Why is the patient telling me this?") and to begin to find their own answers. Fleming implies that these types of learning occur sequentially as the intern begins to feel more confidence as a psychotherapist. Schlessinger (1966), however, comments that implicit in the therapist's attaining the goals of learning as Fleming has outlined them is the ideal of a personal analysis for the student therapist.

Actually, quite a significant body of literature has emerged relatively recently discussing various aspects of the supervisory process, which has come to be viewed as a fascinating phenomenon in itself. Most of the articles published about supervision have been written by supervisors for supervisors; however, it seems important to this author that students be made aware of what has been discovered in the research and what, exactly, is involved in being part of a supervisory relationship. In 1955, Searles published a landmark paper identifying an important process often evident in psychoanalytically oriented supervision, which he termed the process of reflection. This process later came to be referred to as the *parallel process* when Eckstein and Wallerstein first published their book *The Teaching and Learning of Psychotherapy* in 1958 and it was later researched in depth by Doehrman (1976) in her doctoral dissertation. In essence, the reflection or parallel process implies that the therapist may act out, or dramatize, in some way the dynamics of the therapy hour within the supervision hour. In this way the therapist reflects to the supervisor what has happened with the patient or causes a parallel process to occur in the supervision hour; that is, parallel to what occurred in the therapy hour. This acting out may be subtle, as, for example, when the student therapist asks to cancel a supervision session when the patient has canceled their therapy appointment and the supervisor may collude with this request. The acting out may be gross as when the student therapist actually behaves in the supervisory hour in the exact manner that the patient behaves in the therapy (e.g., being aggressive to the supervisor, being withholding from the supervisor), as an unconscious way of showing the supervisor what it is like to be treating this particular patient. As Searles states it: "The processes at work currently in the relationship between patient and therapist are often reflected in the relationship between therapist and supervisor" (p. 135). This, of course, yields very vital and rich material in the supervision, if it can be clearly identified and understood.

One of the methods that is useful in deciding whether this phenomenon is occurring is if the supervisor is able to tap into what he or she is feeling during the supervision. This is countertransference in the sense of being a partly unconscious response to the student therapist and their interaction with the patient, but not necessarily in the sense of tying into the supervisor's own past.

> The emotions experienced by a supervisor—including even his private, "subjective" fantasy experiences and his personal feelings about the supervisee—often provide valuable clarification of processes currently characterizing the relationship between the supervisee and the patient. In addition, these processes are often the very ones causing difficulty in the therapeutic relationship . . . [Searles, 1955, p. 135].

More recently, Gorkin (1987) has written an excellent chapter on countertransference in supervision, acknowledging the emotional phenomena that arise within supervisors as they engage in the supervisory process.

These parallel processes can flow in both directions, that is from the patient "upward" through the therapist to the supervisor and from the supervisor "downward" so that the patient is affected. Often supervisors, because of their own narcissistic needs to help, to teach, to be admired, to be emulated, and to know all the answers may get caught up with their supervisees in these processes and may be unable to interpret them for long periods of time.

That there is an intense and important relationship in supervision has now become better known and accepted. Doehrman's (1976) hypothesis was that anything that happens in the supervisor–therapist relationship, whether positive or negative, would affect the therapist's work with their patients. She looked at the intense transference reactions that therapists have to their supervisors and tried to assess the effects of these transferences on the way they conducted psychotherapy. She concluded that if the conflicts in the supervisory relationship are not resolved there, they will be acted out with patients. Gediman and Wolkenfeld (1980), who refer to the supervisor–therapist–patient relationship as a triadic system, have described shifts during supervision between the objective reporting of data and the enacting of the treatment experience. They confirm that during supervision, "supervisees manifest toward their supervisors many psychic patterns which parallel processes that are prominent in their interactions with their patients. The reverse influence is also observed: analyst and patient re-enact events of the supervisory situation" (p. 234).

The method of using tape-recorded therapy sessions in supervision may sometimes preclude some of the possibilities of parallel processes emerging. In this way, the tapes present a limitation, if we regard the eruption of the parallel process in the supervisory hour as an additional source of information about the therapy. For example, a young male intern I was supervising, Mr. H, was seeing a woman in treatment who happened to be the same age as me. This, we thought, would constitute a parallel process if ever there was one, as here was this poor young man caught between two middle-aged, as it happened, somewhat assertive women. However, no significant parallel process of this type occurred, at least none that we were conscious of. Because all the sessions were taped, Mr. H did not have the opportunity to report from memory; however, he certainly reacted affectively to struggles with the patient and appeared able to talk about his countertransference, which related more to the content of the patient's material (in other words, extreme abuse), in quite a free manner. I was still supervising Mr. H while I was writing this book, so I asked him about the seeming lack of the parallel process phenomenon in our sessions. He replied that because of the tapes and our subsequent discussions of them, he felt I had heard and understood a significant part of his countertransference reaction to this patient and did not feel the need to communicate it as much by acting it out.

There have been several times with other students whose tapes I have listened to, however, when I have seen examples of the parallel process. I am thinking particularly of one student, Ms. J, usually quite reserved in her manner, who discussed her patient in a very animated and excited way in the supervisory sessions. Initially I felt this must be a defensive posture until, in listening to several more of her sessions, I realized that her patient spoke very quickly and excitedly. Once this was identified and we discussed it in more depth, Ms. J became aware that she had felt overwhelmed by her patient's pace which was so different from her own, and was worried that she would not be able to remember and respond appropriately to all of what her patient was saying during the session. In fact, it felt like her patient was making a demand on her that she could not meet, and by talking excitedly to me, she was turning that demand over to me to see what I would do with it. The discussion in the supervisory session was then directed to this process. To quote Searles (1955), in the parallel process "the therapist ... is unconsciously trying to express something about what is going on in the patient—something which the therapist's own anxiety prevents him from putting his finger upon and consciously describing to the supervisor. It is as if the therapist were unconsciously trying, in this fashion, to tell the supervisor what the therapeutic problem is" (p. 144).

The other issue which has emerged in the literature on the supervisory relationship, and which certainly is evident in practice, is what has been called the *teach or trust* dilemma. Because the supervisee is in the role of needing help from a more experienced psychotherapist, and because the therapist–patient relationship inevitably evokes countertransference reactions in the student therapist, there is a natural tendency for the student to begin to talk more personally to the supervisor. Whether or not the student is in psychoanalysis or psychotherapy, this still seems to be the case. Generally, although strictures are expressed against pursuing personal issues in supervision, as Lesser (1983) has stated, it seems that, at some level, the importance of providing a supervisory structure in which some intimate matters may be explored is implicitly recognized.

Most supervisors feel that once the student is apprised of those countertransference reactions that are interfering with the treatment, these reactions do not have to be analyzed or worked through in the supervisory session. Rather they can be talked about in personal therapy or thought through consciously so that errors or failures in empathy because of these conflicts are less likely to occur. There are some supervisors, unfortunately, who appear to encourage a more "therapeutic" mode with their supervisees, possibly under the guise of discussing the student's countertransference, and who use this as a method to get to know the student quickly, to gain power over the student, to satisfy their own curiosity, or to satisfy their need to be seen as "helpful." On the other hand, as Hunt (1981) has said, there are

USING SUPERVISION

supervisors who go to the other extreme and adopt an almost phobic attitude toward the student's countertransference out of a concern that from their position of authority, they may inappropriately intrude into the student's inner life or out of a fear that the supervision will turn into psychotherapy. The best solution seems to lie somewhere in between. It is necessary that the student therapist feel free enough to talk about those parts of his or her personality that are affected by and may interfere with the therapy, but without turning supervision into treatment.

One other factor that has not been discussed in depth in the literature that should be mentioned here is the *student's* need for therapy from the supervisor. There are times, because of the idealizing transference that may occur in the supervisory relationship or because of a particular student's life situation, that the fantasy of being the supervisor's patient may be extremely appealing. For example, one of my supervisees, whose office happened to be located across the hall from mine, confessed to me one day that when she saw patients coming in and out of my office she wished she could be one of them. This is not unexpected because of the above-mentioned factors which facilitate this kind of wishful thinking. Also, by being the patient, the student is taken out of the evaluatory aspect of the relationship and left with only the nurturing "expert" help that may be longed for. Therefore, it is important that you become as aware as possible of your own agenda in supervision as the relationship with your supervisor begins to develop.

One of the aspects of the supervisory relationship that sometimes does not parallel the treatment relationship is the fact that there is a clear teacher–pupil component where, because a certain amount of didactic instruction has to be provided, the teacher–supervisor is more sanctioned than the therapist to give advice, offer interpretations, and in general, spread one's knowledge around. In fact, supervision is often quite gratifying for supervisors because they are permitted to hold forth with students in a way that they cannot with their patients. Unfortunately, sometimes we do not behave in supervision in the manner we know to be the best way of listening in order to understand empathically. In a book chapter that certainly made this supervisor wince entitled "The Empathic Vantage Point in Supervision," Sloane (1986) makes the novel suggestion that supervisors act in supervision the way we hope our students will act as psychotherapists, by listening to our students empathically and doing very little of the talking. He tried suspending his tendency toward theorizing and interpreting, despite the responsibility he felt to inculcate knowledge into his supervisees, and allowed himself to float with the material being presented, letting himself react emotionally and in fantasy. "At crucial moments, and sometimes even for prolonged periods, the empathic point of view [in supervision] may be the only one that will allow access to an affectively comprehensible grasp of the situation the [student] faces with his patient, which is always significantly different from the situation the supervisor would face with the same patient" (p. 191). The dilemma for the supervisor, then, is to teach while providing a role-model of how to listen. If the student therapist does not feel that he or she is getting enough airtime in the supervisory hour, this needs to be raised with the supervisor.

As was mentioned earlier, most of the articles written about supervision have been written from the perspective of supervisors and much of the supervision experience from the point of view of the supervisee is undoubtedly missed. That students feel they need to present an impressive front to their supervisors while still being able to report their difficulties with their patients sometimes requires a fair amount of interpersonal juggling. There are some students who will "solve" this dilemma for themselves by only presenting positive material from the session that shows how well the patient is moving along and how the therapist is conducting the therapy consistent with the supervisor's theoretical and therapeutic stance. Of course, very little can be learned from this type of presentation. Other students will only present negative data, partly as a cry for help from the supervisor and partly to defend against the possibility that their supervisor may criticize them, and therefore they criticize themselves first. Again minimal learning is achieved.

One of the difficulties that seems, unfortunately, to be innate to being a supervisee is that student therapists will sometimes find themselves in the situation of interacting with their patients in a way that they either do not understand or do not agree with, simply because they "know" that this is the way their supervisor wants them to interact. There had been almost no literature written from the supervisee's point of view, with the exception of a study of beginning psychiatric residents carried out by Tischler (1968), until a rare article actually written by a supervisee, Gauthier, appeared in 1984. In this article, Gauthier describes how the student therapist must place themselves in "the role of a messenger" bringing the supervisor's words to the patient. It certainly is difficult to arrive at your session with your patient filled with material from your last meeting with your supervisor, without having integrated your supervisor's comments. If you do not understand why your supervisor has said what they said, or if you do not agree but your supervisor instructs you to do as they say anyway, then the subsequent interaction with your patient of course feels very unnatural. Ideally, supervisors should try to give understanding and advice that is congruent with the student therapist's personality and the way that is most comfortable for that person to conduct therapy. However, this cannot always be expected. It may be that your supervisor is unaware that you are very uncomfortable with a certain approach, in which case it is your responsibility to inform him or her about this, and to negotiate a reasonable solution. It also may be that what you feel in your gut may not be the most appropriate way to proceed with your patient at this time and may lead you into more difficulties later which your supervisor can foresee. Again, negotiating and explaining have to become part of the supervisory process so that, although at times you may not totally agree, you can rationalize trying out what your supervisor has suggested, if for no other reason than just to see what effect it has on the psychotherapy. This process of rationalization will help you to come across as more consonant with your patient. In terms of the impotence student therapists sometimes feel, Gauthier describes rather poignantly a clinical vignette wherein he was treating a difficult patient and not getting much help in his supervision toward the bolstering of his confidence in himself as a therapist. At one point in the treatment, his patient brought him a gift. He states: "I brought the gift, intact, to the supervisor. As I often had the feeling that the real therapeutic relationship was more between him and my patient than between me and her (or at least that it should be, for the patient's sake), wasn't the gift addressed more to him than to me?" (p. 515).

Despite what has been said above, most supervisors do not expect the supervisee to take back to the patient a word-for-word, or even close to that, interpretation or other observation discussed in the supervision meeting. The goal of the supervision is to provide a *general understanding* of the process of the psychotherapy and the psychodynamics of the patient. Taking too literally what your supervisor has said will not be beneficial to you or your patient. It often happens, for example, that the topic you discuss with your supervisor (i.e., that your patient has described in the preceding session) is not the topic that the patient raises in the next session. Even if, on rare occasions, you feel that your supervisor has come up with a brilliant interpretation of something your patient did in the previous session, keep in mind that the chances are that this interpretation will not be

USING SUPERVISION

able to be given in the very next session. Therefore, you will have to hold it in your mental file and clear your head of your supervision, at least to some extent, so that you can listen to your patient all over again. If you enter your postsupervisory therapy session with your supervisory introject making comments in your head about the previous session, then you risk being experienced by your patient as noticeably unempathic. It is best to try to take some time after supervision to integrate what has been discussed with your supervisor with what you already know about your patient; then, if necessary, you can attempt to get a revised overall picture of your patient, adding in the new insights from the supervision meeting.

All of the following questions constitute dilemmas that we somehow expect beginning students to be able to solve: How much do you keep your supervisor in your head when you are in your therapy session with your patient? How much do you listen to your supervisor's way of doing psychotherapy if it does not feel consonant with your own style? How often do you not respond to your patient spontaneously without first checking with your supervisor? Managing these sorts of problems gets easier with experience, both experience in doing psychotherapy and experience in being supervised; but it is particularly difficult at first. These kinds of issues can also, like other issues about being a therapist, be discussed with your supervisor, who may be able to give you concrete examples of when certain behaviors are appropriate and when they are not.

The timing of the supervisory session can also be an important factor. From my experience, it seems best not to schedule supervision immediately after the psychotherapy session, as this tends to encourage "ventilation" by the student, rather than thoughtful commentary on the psychotherapy. Even worse is scheduling the supervision for the hour before the next therapy session. This is extremely confusing for the student who is still dealing with the last psychotherapy session and the supervisor's reaction to it when going into the next one, and has had no time to digest the discussion. It will be almost impossible to listen to the patient under these circumstances.

One of the parallel processes in supervision and therapy that has been alluded to earlier in this book is that the ending of the student therapist's psychotherapy with their patient may also signal the termination of the supervisory relationship. Here again the intern is in the middle of two emotionally charged situations. Often the termination of the supervisory relationship is dealt with vicariously in supervision by discussing the patient's feelings about stopping treatment and the therapist's feelings about ending therapy with the patient. The ending of the supervision itself is not discussed in any great detail. However, since the possible intensity of this relationship with its many transference opportunities has been acknowledged, the ending of the supervision relationship should be viewed as significant as well. The issues that relate to termination in therapy, that is, issues of separation and loss, and of growing up, are an integral part of the ending of the supervisory relationship.

For some students, the ending of a particular supervisory relationship may come as a relief, as they feel that they no longer have to account for their every word in therapy and that they are no longer being assessed and evaluated. Particularly if the relationship has been intense and the negative transferences have not been able to be worked through, or in reality there has been a bad match, then the student may feel like they have been let out of school and that they are now free to go their own way. If the relationship has been one characterized by dependency, the student therapist may feel uneasy or even frightened about going out alone into the professional world. You will perhaps be glad to know that very often both students and their supervisors feel sad to say good-bye to each other. They see the relationship as having been mutually rewarding and one in which each one has learned from the other. Often they have developed a bond of mutual respect and a comfortable way of relating to each other. And often each has enhanced the other's self-esteem and sense of professionalism. It is important and helpful to both the student and the supervisor to allow for time for the discussion of at least some of these feelings before the ending of the supervision occurs.

And so we have come to the ending of this book which, it is hoped, will have provided an interesting beginning to your becoming a psychotherapist. Of all the professions, this one—at once scientific and enigmatic—demands the most of its practitioners as human beings: It will challenge your intellect, your emotions, and your personal philosophy of life as no other profession will.

References

American Psychiatric Association (1986), *Diagnostic and Statistical Manual of Mental Disorders* (DSM-III-R), 3rd ed. rev. Washington, DC: American Psychiatric Press.
Baker, R. (1980), The finding "not suitable" in the selection of supervised cases. *Internat. Rev. Psycho-Anal.*, 7:353–363.
Basch, M. F. (1980), *Doing Psychotherapy.* New York: Basic Books.
Beier, E. G. (1964), On supervision in psychotherapy. *Psychotherapy*, 1:91–95.
Berger, D. M. (1987), *Clinical Empathy.* Northvale, NJ: Jason Aronson.
Bibring, G. L. (1968), *The Teaching of Dynamic Psychiatry.* New York: International Universities Press.
Breuer, J., & Freud, S. (1893–1895), Studies on Hysteria. *Standard Edition*, 2. London: Hogarth Press, 1955.
Castelnuovo-Tedesco, P. (1991), *Dynamic Psychiatry.* Madison, CT: International Universities Press.
Claghorn, J. L., ed. (1976), *Successful Psychotherapy.* New York: Brunner/Mazel.
Doehrman, M. J. G. (1976), Parallel process in supervision and psychotherapy. *Bull. Menninger Clinic*, 40/1:1–104.
Eagle, M. (1984), *Recent Developments in Psychoanalysis: A Critical Evaluation.* New York: McGraw-Hill.
Ekstein, R., & Wallerstein, R. S. (1958), *The Teaching and Learning of Psychotherapy.* New York: International Universities Press, 1972.
Fleming, J. (1953), The role of supervision in psychiatric training. *Bull. Menninger Clinic*, 17:157–169.
Freud, S. (1900), The Interpretation of Dreams. *Standard Edition*, 4 & 5. London: Hogarth Press, 1953.
—— (1912a), The dynamics of transference. *Standard Edition*, 12:99–108. London: Hogarth Press, 1958.
—— (1912b), Recommendations to physicians practicing psychoanalysis. *Standard Edition*, 12:109–120. London: Hogarth Press, 1955.
—— (1914), Remembering, repeating and working-through. *Standard Edition*, 12:145–156. London: Hogarth Press, 1955.

REFERENCES

———— (1917), Introductory lectures on psycho-analysis. *Standard Edition*, 12:431–447. London: Hogarth Press, 1963.
———— (1921), Group psychology and the analysis of the ego. *Standard Edition*, 18:67–143. London: Hogarth Press, 1955.
———— (1924), An autobiographical study. *Standard Edition*, 20:1–74. London: Hogarth Press.
Frosch, J. (1990), *Psychodynamic Psychiatry: Theory and Practice*, Vols. 1 & 2. Madison, CT: International Universities Press.
Gabbard, G. O. (1990), *Psychodynamic Psychiatry in Clinical Practice*. Washington, DC: American Psychiatric Press.
Gauthier, M. (1984), Countertransference and supervision: A discussion of some dynamics from the point of view of the supervisee. *Can. J. Psychiatry*, 29:513–519.
Gediman, H. K., & Wolkenfeld, F. (1980), The parallelism phenomenon in psychoanalysis and supervision: Its reconsideration as a triadic system. *Psychoanal. Quart.*, 49:234–255.
Gorkin, M. (1987), *The Uses of Countertransference*. New York: Jason Aronson.
Greenberg, J. R., & Mitchell, S. (1983), *Object Relations in Psychoanalytic Theory*. Cambridge, MA: Harvard University Press.
Greenson, R. R. (1967), *The Technique and Practice of Psychoanalysis*, Vol. 1. New York: International Universities Press.
Hildebrandt, F. W. (1875), Der traum und seine verwerthung fur leben, in Freud (1900), *Standard Edition*, 4:62–63. London: Hogarth Press, 1953.
Hunt, W. (1981), The use of the countertransference in psychotherapy supervision. *J. Amer. Acad. Psychoanal.*, 9/3:361–373.
Hutt, M. L. (1953), Discussion of problems in supervision and training in clinical psychology. *Amer. J. Orthopsychiatry*, 23:328–331.
Kelly, G. A. (1951), Principles of training in clinical psychology. *Amer. J. Orthopsychiatry*, 21:312–318.
Knight, R. P. (1945), Training in psychotherapy and psychoanalysis. *Bull. Menninger Clinic*, 9:54–59.
Kohut, H. (1977), *The Restoration of the Self*. New York: International Universities Press.
Kubie, L. S. (1958), Research into the process of supervision in psychoanalysis. *Psychoanal. Quart.*, 27:226–236.
Lesser, R. M. (1983), Supervision: Illusions, anxieties and questions. *Contemp. Psychoanal.*, 19/1:120–129.

REFERENCES

MacKinnon, R. A., & Michels, M. (1971), *The Psychiatric Interview in Clinical Practice*. Philadelphia: W. B. Saunders.

Racker, H. (1968), *Transference and Countertransference*. London: Hogarth Press.

Sandler, J., Dare, C., & Holder, A. (1973), *The Patient and the Analyst: The Basis of the Psychoanalytic Process*. New York: International Universities Press.

Schlessinger, N. (1966), Supervision of psychotherapy: A critical review of the literature. *Arch. Gen. Psychiatry*, 15:129–134.

Schwartz, E. K., & Abel, T. M. (1955), The professional education of the psychoanalytic psychotherapist. *Amer. J. Psychotherapy*, 9:253–261.

Searles, H. F. (1955), The informational value of the supervisor's emotional experiences. *Psychiatry*, 18:135–146.

Slavson, S. R. (1953), Sources of countertransference and group-induced anxiety. *Internat. J. Group Psychotherapy*, 3:373–388.

Sloane, J. A. (1986), The empathic vantage point in supervision. In: *Progress in Self Psychology*, Vol. 2, ed. A. Goldberg. New York: Guilford Press, pp. 188–211.

Sterba, R. F. (1929), The dynamics of the dissolution of the transference resistance. *Psychoanal. Quart.*, 9:363–379.

Tischler, G. L. (1968), The beginning resident and supervision. *Arch. Gen. Psychiat.*, 19:418–422.

Wagner, F. F. (1957), Supervision of psychotherapy. *Amer. J. Psychotherapy*, 11:759–768.

Winnicott, D. W. (1945), Primitive emotional development. In: *Through Paediatrics to Psycho-Analysis*. London: Hogarth Press, 1958.

Woody, R. H., & Robertson, M. (1988), *Becoming a Clinical Psychologist*. Madison, CT: International Universities Press.

Name Index

Abel, T. M., 137

Baker, R., 58
Basch, M. F., 3–4, 29, 95–96, 112–113
Berger, D. M., 5, 99
Bibring, G. L., xii
Breuer, J., 6–7

Castelnuovo-Tedesco, P., xii, 20
Claghorn, J. L., 15–16

Dare, C., xii
Doehrman, M. J. G., 140, 142

Eagle, M., xii
Eckstein, R., 140

Fleming, J., 139–140
Freud, S., 1–2, 4, 6–7, 9–10, 12–13, 20, 65, 79–80
Frosch, J., xii, 2

Gabbard, G. O., xii, 25
Gauthier, M., 147–148
Gediman, H. K., 142
Gorkin, M., 141
Greenberg, J. R., xii
Greenson, R. R., xii, 2, 7, 8, 10, 15, 17, 18, 20, 70, 86, 125

Hildebrandt, F. W., 79–80

Hunt, W., 144–145
Hutt, M. L., 137

Kelly, G. A., 137
Knight, R. P., 137
Kohut, H., 4
Kubie, L. S., 139

Lesser, R. M., 144
Luborsky, 15–16

MacKinnon, R. A., 13
Michels, M., xii, 13
Mitchell, S., xii

Racker, H., 13
Robertson, M., 3

Sandler, J., xii
Schlessinger, N., 140
Schwartz, E. K., 137
Searles, H. F., 140–141, 143–144
Slavson, S. R., 13–14
Sloane, J. A., 146
Sterba, R. F., 15

Tischler, G. L., 147

Wagner, F. F., 137
Wallerstein, R. S., 140
Winnicott, D. W., 16
Wolkenfeld, F., 142
Woody, R. H., 3

Subject Index

Acting out, 22
   during termination, 115
Affective involvement, resistance and, 22
Aggression, 129–130
"Aha!" responses, 25
Alcohol abuse, 44
Anger, difficulty controlling, 56–57
Anonymity, 125
Avoidance behavior, 128–129

Behavior change, 89–90

Caretaking patient, 131–132
Challenges, special, 121–136
Change, fear of, 20
Chief complaint, 31–32
   exploration of, 32
Corrective learning, 139–140
Countertransference, 53–54
   definition of, 13–15
   negative, 14
   with older patient, 132–133
   with patient who seems like you, 133–134
   positive, 14
   with seductive patient, 126–127
   in supervisory sessions, 141, 143–145
Creative learning, 140
Crisis situation, 61

Defenses, 20–21

Dependency, 130
Depression, questions to ask about, 34–35
Diagnosis, postulation of, 49–50
Displacement, 87–88
   discovery of, 86
   inappropriate, 8
Dreams
   associations to, 81, 83
   case history of, 81–82
   interpretation of, 79–80
   significance of, 82–84
Drug abuse, 44

Empathic failure, 6
Empathy, 4–6
   definition of, 4
   difficulty of, 65
   in first session, 32–33

Fantasies, aggressive, 129
Father, questions to ask about, 41
Flight, 22
Formulation, 48–51
Free association, 78–79
Free-floating attention, 65

Grateful patient, 130

Heterosexual relationships, 43
Historic approach, 3–4
History
   flagging transference in, 46–48

SUBJECT INDEX

formal or structured, 40
History taking
  on alcohol/drug use, 44
  on close relatives, 42
  on father, 41
  on leaving home, 42–43
  on medical problems, 44
  mental status in, 44–45
  on mother, 41
  on previous counseling experience, 44
  on relationships, 43–44
  on school life, 42
  on siblings, 42
  time frame for, 45–46
  on working life, 43
Holding environment, 16–17
Holiday, separation during, 92–96
Home, leaving of, 42–43
  guilt feelings about, 48
Homosexual relationships, 43
Humor, as defense, 125–126

Idealization, strained, 123
Imitative learning, 139
Impulse delay, 56
Initial interview, 28–38
  ending of, 36–37
  information gathered from, 32–34
  patient's reaction to, 39–40
Interpretation
  definition of, 18–19
  resistance to, 19
  when and how to use, 73–75
  in working through, 25
Interpretation of Dreams, The, 79–80
Introductory Lectures, on resistance, 20
Intrusiveness, 124–125

Language, psychodynamic psychotherapy, 1–26
Learning, in supervision experience, 139–140
Listening, empathic, 32–33, 65

Mental status, 44–45
Mother, questions to ask about, 41

Narcissism, defenses of, 21
Neurotic conflict, study of, 1–2
Non sequiturs, 78
Note-taking, 37–38

Observation, 18

Parallel process, 140–144, 150
Parents
  ability to let go of, 46
  "good," 46
  marriage of, 41
  patient's view of marriage of, 47–48
Passive aggression, 21
Patient
  "bright," 121–122
  caretaking, 131–132
  condescending, 123–124
  "dumb," 123
  entertaining, 125–126
  feelings about hospital for outpatient treatment, 29–31
  first response to, 53–54
  greeting of, 28–29
  information to learn about, in initial interview, 32–34
  initial interview of, 28–38
  intrusive, 124–125
  like you, 133–134

making comfortable, 29
motivation of, 39–40
older, 132–133
overly grateful/ungrateful, 130–131
"perfect," 134–136
psychological mindedness of, 54–55
reaction of, to first session, 39–40
reasons of, for seeking treatment, 31
"scary," 129–130
seductive, 126–127
selection of, 53–62
signs of bad candidate for psychodynamic psychotherapy, 57–62
signs of good candidate for psychodynamic psychotherapy, 55–57
silences of, 75–78
special challenges of, 121–136
termination issues raised by, 101
therapist's reaction to, 67–69
tolerance of unstructured situation, 54
understanding of, 70–73
who wants to leave too soon, 128–129
who will not leave, 127–128
Patient history, understanding of, 3–4
Patient-therapist relationship. *See* Therapist-patient relationship
"Perfect" patient, 134–136
Posttermination phase, 113–114
Presenting problem, 31–32
Progress notes, 38

Projections, 86
Psychoanalysis, versus psychodynamic psychotherapies, 2
Psychodynamic psychotherapy
  definition and basis of, 1–3
  as historic approach, 3–4
  language of, 1–26
  patient selection for, 54–62
  signs of bad candidate for, 57–62
  signs of good candidate for, 55–57
  starting out in, 27–38
Psychological mindedness, 54–55
Psychological tests, interpretation of, 2–3
Psychotherapy
  change in approach to, 60–61
  difficulty of getting started in, 64
  educating patient about, 36
  middle phase of, 64–97
  origins and characteristics of, 2–3
  progression of, 84–85
  structured vs. unstructured approach of, 61
Psychotic symptomology, 55
Psychotic thinking, 57–58

Referrals
  good and bad, 27
  during termination phase, 115–116
Relationships
  impoverished, 59–60
  patient's view of, 47–48
  questions to ask about, 43–44
Resistance, 19
  awareness of, 22–23
  in context of patient's life, 23
  definition of, 20–24
  interpretation of, 23–24

SUBJECT INDEX

silence as, 75, 76
unconscious, 21–22
Rorschach test, 2–3

School life, questions to ask about, 42
Seductive patient, 126–127
Self-depreciating behavior, 123
Separation
 guilt feelings about, 48
 patient's dealing with, 46–47
 on vacation or holiday, 92–96
Sessions
 being late for, 21–22
 ending of, 17
 ending of first, 36–37
 final, 105–106
 first, 28–38
 missing of, 112
 taking of notes during, 37–38
 tape-recorded, 142–144
 taping of, xii-xiii
Sexual relationships, issues of, 48
Sibling transference, 47
Siblings, questions to ask about, 42
Silence, 63
 breaking of, 77
 patterns of, 77–78
 understanding of, 75–78
Stereotype plates, 7
Studies on Hysteria, on transference, 6–7
Suicidal thoughts, exploration of, 35–36
Supervision, 61–62, 137–151
 countertransference in, 141
 ending of, 150–151
 getting what you need from, 147–149
 need for therapy from, 145

parallel processes in, 142–144, 150
process of, 138, 140–141
from student view, 146–147
use of tape-recorded therapy sessions in, 142–144
Supervisor-student relationship, 138
 intensity of, 142
 paralleling treatment relationship, 145–146
Supervisor-therapist-patient relationship, 142
Supervisory sessions
 contract of, 139
 countertransference in, 143–145
 learning in, 139–140
 structure of, 138
 timing of, 149–150

Tape-recorded sessions, 142–144
Teach or trust dilemma, 144
Teaching and Learning of Psychotherapy, The, 140–141
Termination, 99–119
 acting out during, 115
 case history of, 106–108
 decision for, 99–100
 fantasies about, 102
 as learning opportunity, 112–113
 natural, 100–101
 negotiation of, 104–105
 new issues during, 103, 110–111
 premature, 108–109, 111–112
 prolonged vs. condensed, 109–110
 resistance to, 104
 setting date for, 103–104
 with student therapists, 109
 transference during, 114–119
Termination note, 113
Therapeutic alliance. *See* Working alliance

[162]

SUBJECT INDEX

Therapist
  anonymity of, 125
  balance between emotions and cognition in, 69–70
  empathic, 4–6
  identification with, 16
  impact of, on patient, 86–87
  meeting outside therapy, 90–92
  prejudices of, 13–14
  reaction of, to patient, 67–69
  self-confidence of, 27
  starting out, 27–38
  vacation of, 92–96
Therapist-patient relationship
  as friendship, 117–118
  transference and, 6–7, 87–88
  transference in, 6–7
  working alliance and, 15–18
Therapy. See also Psychodynamic psychotherapy; Psychotherapy
  termination of, 99–119
  transitions in, 40, 63–64
Transference
  behavior change in, 89–90
  definition of, 6–12
  flagging of, during termination, 114–119
  flagging of, in history, 46–48
  flagging of, in ongoing therapy, 85–97
  indications of, 86–87
  lack of positive relationships and, 60
  manifested in patient's life, 11–12
  maternal and paternal, 10–11
  negative, 10, 11
  positive, 9–10, 11
  resistance and, 22–23
  separation during holiday/vacations and, 92–96
  sibling, 47
  technique of handling, 7
  triggers of, 90–91
  understanding of, 3
Transference neurosis, 12–13
Transitions, 40
  to ongoing therapy, 63–64
Treatment recommendation, 53

Unconscious, dreams and, 79–82
Ungrateful patient, 130–131
Unstructured therapy, 54

Vacation
  separation during, 92–96
  telling patient about, 95–96

Working alliance
  definition of, 15–18
  establishment of, 36
  facilitation of, 65
  formation of, 65–68
Working life, questions to ask about, 43
Working through, 24–26

[163]